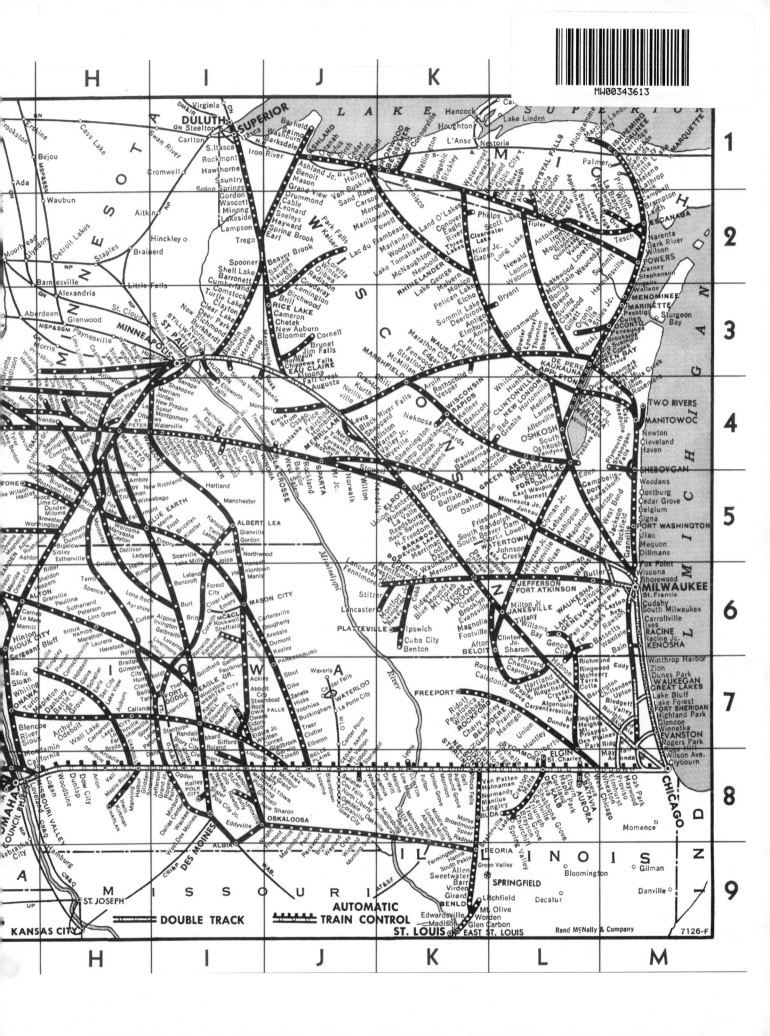

DOUBLE TRACK

AUTOMATIC TRAIN CONTROL

Rand McNally & Company

7126-F

CHICAGO & NORTH

FREIGHT TRAINS AND

PATRICK C. DORIN

WESTERN

The Overland Route

EXW	10-5	H 13-7
EW	9-4	H 14-5
IL	40-6	
IW	9-2	
IH	10-6	
BLT 3-45	CU FT 3902	

EQUIPMENT

TLC
PUBLISHING INC.

2003
TLC Publishing, Inc.
1387 Winding Creek Lane
Lynchburg, Virginia 24503-3776

International Standard Book Number   1-883089-85-9
Library of Congress Control Number   2003103898

Design and production by
Kevin J. Holland
type&DESIGN
Burlington, Ontario

Produced on the MacOS™

Printed by
Walsworth Publishing Company
Marceline, Missouri 64658

OTHER BOOKS BY PATRICK C. DORIN FROM TLC—

The Challenger
Chicago & North Western Passenger Service—The Postwar Years
Chicago & North Western Passenger Equipment
Louisville & Nashville Passenger Trains—The Pan-American Era (with Charles Castner and Bob Chapman)
Louisville & Nashville—The Old Reliable (with Charles Castner and Ron Flanary)
Michigan–Ontario Iron Ore Railroads
Minnesota–Ontario Iron Ore Railroads
Missouri Pacific Freight Trains and Equipment
Missouri Pacific Passenger Trains—The Postwar Years
Western Pacific Locomotives and Cars

FRONT COVER—
With General Electric DASH8-40C No. 8514 on the head end, a C&NW coal train heads east at Logan, Wyoming, on September 3, 1981. (Lou Schmitz)

TITLE PAGE—
Forty-foot box car 82540 (series 81452-84250) was built in 1945 by General American. It carried slogans for the "Overland Route" on one side and "Route of the *400* Streamliners" on the other. (GATC, Author's Collection)

Dedicated to the Memory
of
Larry Burlaga

Professional Railroader,
Railroad Enthusiast, Historian,
and Devoted Family Man

THE AUTHOR

Patrick C. Dorin has been interested in railroads since the age of two.

While attending undergraduate school at Northland College, he worked for the Great Northern Railway. Later he worked for the Elgin, Joliet & Eastern Railway, the Duluth, Missabe & Iron Range, and the Milwaukee Road. His employment in the railroad industry included positions in operations, marketing research, customer service, and cost accounting.

He holds degrees in business administration, marketing, elementary education, and school administration including a Ph.D. from the University of Minnesota.

He recently retired as a school principal for the Superior, Wisconsin, schools and has taught marketing, operations research, transportation, Japanese culture, and school administration courses on a part-time basis for both the University of Wisconsin–Superior and the University of Minnesota–Duluth.

Railroads continue to hold a strong fascination for Pat, and he has published over 30 books and nearly 30 articles on aspects of railroad service, companies, and equipment, as well as other subjects.

Pat Dorin lives in Superior, Wisconsin, with his wife Karen.

ACKNOWLEDGMENTS

This book on C&NW freight trains, service and equipment was actually started 30 years ago and was to be part of the author's first book on the C&NW, published in 1971. Here we are over three decades later, and the C&NW has become part of the "Fallen Flags" category.

Many people provided a great deal of assistance, insights, and photographs for this project. The book would not have been possible without the wide variety of contributions that the following people were so willing to provide to the author.

Thanks go to the many people of the former C&NW's Public Relations, Operating, and Marketing Departments, and to companies such as Thrall Car, ACF, and General American Transportation Corporation which provided equipment photos to the C&NW for their information and historical record.

Thanks also are extended to the C&NW Historical Society, and more specifically to Joe Piersen, Dale Kuhn, Joe Follmar, and Charles Stats of that organization.

The following people provided a wide diversity of photographs and illustrations:

Bob Lorenz, William S. Kuba, Harold K. Vollrath, Thomas Dorin, Michael Dorin, Fred Ziebe, David R. Carlson, Jim Scribbins, William A. Raia, Al Paterson (Paterson-George Collection), Robert C. Anderson, Michael Burlaga, Lou Schmitz, Dan Mackey, Dennis Roos, Kevin J. Holland, and Joel Nagro.

I cannot thank these individuals enough because as mentioned previously, the book would not have been possible without their kind and thoughtful assistance and the photographic artwork covering over 50 years from the 1940s through the Union Pacific merger—and even a bit beyond.

Thank you again, each and everyone!

This freight station listing published by the C&NW in December 1960 included a chart showing all of the North Western's interchange partners at the time. (Author's Collection)

HANDY MAP and LIST OF FREIGHT STATIONS SERVED BY THE NEW CHICAGO AND NORTH WESTERN RAILWAY

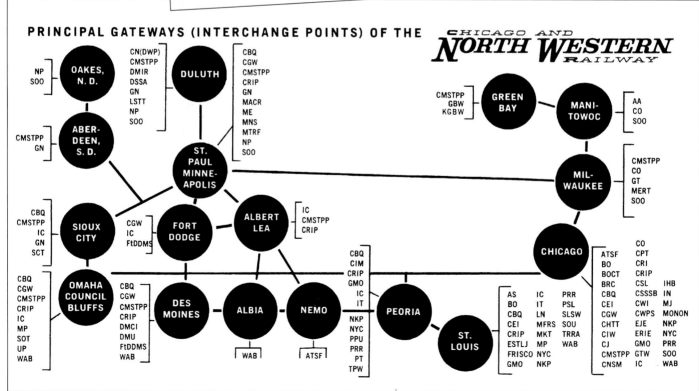

PRINCIPAL GATEWAYS (INTERCHANGE POINTS) OF THE CHICAGO AND NORTH WESTERN RAILWAY

OAKES, N.D. — NP, SOO

DULUTH — CN(DWP), CMSTPP, DMIR, DSSA, GN, LSTT, NP, SOO

ABERDEEN, S.D. — CMSTPP, GN

ST. PAUL MINNEAPOLIS — CBQ, CGW, CMSTPP, CRIP, GN, MACR, ME, MNS, MTRF, NP, SOO

GREEN BAY — CMSTPP, GBW, KGBW

MANITOWOC — AA, CO, SOO

MILWAUKEE — CMSTPP, CO, GT, MERT, SOO

SIOUX CITY — CBQ, CMSTPP, IC, GN, SCT

FORT DODGE — CGW, IC, FtDDMS

ALBERT LEA — IC, CMSTPP, CRIP

OMAHA COUNCIL BLUFFS — CBQ, CGW, CMSTPP, CRIP, IC, MP, SOT, UP, WAB

DES MOINES — CBQ, CGW, CMSTPP, CRIP, DMCI, DMU, FtDDMS, WAB

ALBIA — WAB

NEMO — ATSF

NEMO (list) — CBQ, CIM, CRIP, GMO, IC, IT, NKP, NYC, PPU, PRR, PT, TPW

PEORIA

ST. LOUIS

CHICAGO — ATSF, BO, BOCT, BRC, CBQ, CEI, CGW, CHTT, CIW, CJ, CMSTPP, CNSM, CO, CPT, CRI, CRIP, CSL, CSSSB, CWI, CWPS, EJE, ERIE, GMO, GTW, IC, IHB, IN, MJ, MONON, NKP, NYC, PRR, SOO, WAB

AS, BO, CBQ, CEI, CRIP, ESTLJ, FRISCO, GMO, IC, IT, LN, MFRS, MKT, MP, NYC, NKP, PRR, PSL, SLSW, SOU, TRRA, WAB

viii

INTRODUCTION

The Chicago & North Western was known as a "Granger Road," but the reality is that the company handled a rather interesting and diverse freight traffic mix. Not only did the railroad handle grains and other farm products as a "granger," but it was also a heavy merchandise hauler, particularly with the later intermodal operations, and played a crucial role in the paper industry, forest products, iron ore, and coal. Parts of the railroad are well-known for their role in particular geographic locations, such as the iron ore traffic in Michigan.

The book looks at C&NW freight operations and equipment from the postwar period to the Union Pacific merger in 1995, but there are segments of early history as well as concentrations on the transition period from the 1940s through the early 1980s. There are several reasons for the selection of that time period. First of all, many of us are quite familiar with the trains and the motive power of that period of time—especially from steam to diesel. Many railroad hobbyists model their motive power and rolling stock from this period of time. Secondly, this time period saw some of the greatest changes not only on the C&NW, but on all of the North American railroads.

The Chicago & North Western was a colorful railroad, with its green-and-yellow color schemes that lasted until the UP merger. The company did not throw its public image away as so many other railroads did.

The C&NW was an important partner in the famous Overland Route linking transcontinental freight movements from eastern carriers to the Union Pacific. Intermodal trains even picked up on some of the former passenger train fleet, by adopting train names like the *Viking 400.*

The C&NW's freight car fleet, in most cases, promoted a positive image (except for secondhand cars which were simply stenciled with C&NW reporting marks and left in their previous schemes).

There is much to be learned by reviewing and studying the Chicago & North Western Railway. Many of the concepts could be used in launching new freight services in the 21st century. Who knows what the future will hold as we move further into the 21st century—where only the railroad industry will be able to alleviate both airway and highway traffic congestion with new partnerships in transportation.

Hopefully this book will provide readers with some interesting concepts for modeling and enhance the enjoyment of railroading.

Patrick C. Dorin
Superior, Wisconsin
July 4, 2003

CONTENTS

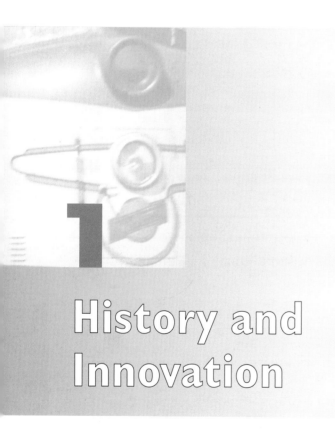

1

History and Innovation

The Chicago & North Western was a very important part of the North American railroad picture from 1848, when predecessor Galena & Chicago Union railroad was launched. This little short line grew and eventually achieved over 10,000 miles of rail lines fanning out from Chicago to Michigan, Minnesota, and westward to the Dakotas and Wyoming. Altogether, the C&NW system consisted of over 135 different corporations within its family tree. Because of the Great Depression, many branch lines were abandoned and by 1948, the route mileage of the Chicago & North Western and the Chicago, St. Paul, Minneapolis & Omaha railroads was at the 9,630 mark. The C&NW operated 8,063 miles, while the "Omaha Road" operated 1,567 miles, or nearly 20 percent of the C&NW system's total mileage.

After World War II, there were two major railroad corporations operated under the C&NW ban-

ner, with the North Western motive power and rolling stock carrying C&NW reporting marks, while the CSt.PM&O (known as the Omaha) carried either the full CStPM&O or CMO reporting marks. The former was common on the motive power and passenger equipment, while the latter was common on the freight equipment. This made for some interesting and delightful train operations especially where the two railroads connected. In fact, the C&NW System operated its freight trains as "through" trains between Chicago and the Twin Cities and between Chicago and the Duluth-Superior terminals.

The C&NW has been classified as a "granger" railroad because of the farming territory served throughout parts of Iowa, Wisconsin, Minnesota, and the Dakotas. However, the territory included industrial areas including Chicago, eastern and central Wisconsin, northern and cen-

tral Illinois, eastern Iowa, and the iron ore ranges in northern Wisconsin and Michigan. This combination made for some rather interesting traffic mixes throughout the system. During the 1940s and well into the 1950s, farm products contributed about 25 percent of the C&NW's total gross revenues.

The railroad began a transition era lasting from the mid-1940s to the mid-1950s in terms of the dieselization program. The transition era, in many ways, continued until the 1990s when one looks at the change from the box car to the 100-ton covered hopper car for the grain traffic. Still other changes took place in the coal traffic flows, such as the addition of the western coal traffic to a variety of power plants on the C&NW as well as being interchanged with eastern railroads. To make things even more interesting, the coal hopper car capacities ranged from the 50- and 70-ton

What symbolizes a railroad company? In many cases, it was (and is) the color scheme on the motive power, freight, and passenger equipment. During the 1940s and 1950s, while the C&NW was in the transition era of dieselization, the green, yellow, and black color scheme with the insignia incorporated in wings on the nose identified the railroad. This C&NW publicity photo proudly promoted the new Electro-Motive F3 freight power. (Author's Collection)

The C&NW added train names on the front of many steam locomotives, like Northern No. 3010. (G.M. Best, Author's Collection)

The C&NW was justly proud of its big Northerns. (Kevin J. Holland Collection)

corporate structure of the changes in the railroad system will be covered in a bit more detail later in this chapter.

The C&NW faced a number of service, equipment, freight car control, and freight rate challengers during the transition period of the 1940s and 1950s. The company came up with a number of solutions that provided some interesting and positive results for the railroad over both the short and long terms.

Wet wood pulp was one of the important traffic commodities during the 1950s. During the winter months, the wet wood pulp was handled in refrigerator cars to keep the cargo from freezing. Many of the wooden refrigerator cars were due for retirement and so the company launched a research program in 1951 to find a solution. It took until February 1953 to create a successful insulated box car, which kept a test wood pulp load from freezing for six days in zero-degree weather.

The railroad remodeled 12 steel-underframe, composite box cars including the test car at its Winona, Minnesota, shops. The 40-foot cars had an interior capacity of 2,576 cubic feet, which was 193 cubic feet larger than the refrigerator cars that would soon be replaced.

Still another freight car innovation arrived on the scene in 1954. The company took a conventional end-bunker refrigerator car built in 1938,

cars to the newer 100-ton-capacity coal cars. The transition era continued.

As the C&NW began to trim more and more branch lines within its territory, the railroad's transition began to cover still other factors. For example, the Omaha Road was leased and folded completely into the C&NW system. The "CMO" reporting marks became a thing of the past. The

Largest Dual Service Locomotive in the World

THE GIANT CLASS "H"

IT is with pleasure we present the Chicago & North Western Railway's latest and finest contribution to the field of modern steam locomotives. A mighty thing is this giant Mogul of the Rails. To appreciate its tremendous power and mammoth size, permit us to point out these facts: The Class "H" weighs nearly twice as much as any locomotive formerly in North Western service; it has a pulling power 50 per cent greater than other passenger engines; is capable of attaining a speed of 85 miles an hour; can haul 150 loaded freight cars (a train about 1½ miles long) at a speed of 50 miles an hour!

The Class "H" is 103 feet 4 inches long and 16 feet high. The main frame and the cylinders for the engine is a single steel casting 58 feet, 3 inches long and weighs 73,000 pounds, no bolts or rivets being used in its assembly. The engine and tender weigh 818,000 pounds. It has sixteen wheels—four front engine truck wheels, eight driving wheels and four

trailer wheels. The diameter of the driving wheels is 76 inches. The tractive power of the Class "H" is 71,800 pounds, with an additional 12,400 from a booster engine for use in starting. The tender has a water capacity of 18,000 gallons and a coal capacity of 20 tons. Steel plates for the tender tank are all welded together and onto a one-piece steel casting which forms the frame and the bottom of the tender tank, no bolts or rivets being used in the construction. There are 35 of these mammoth locomotives now in service on the Chicago & North Western Railway, each representing a cost of $120,000. They perform a dual service, being used either as passenger or freight locomotives . . . and the transition from the one to the other is simply a matter of pulling a lever!

Automatic train control equipment is also a feature of the Class "H". This device automatically stops the train when it approaches another train or slows it to a 20-mile-an-hour speed in restricted areas. Thus safety is assured travelers under all conditions.

Here, then, is an outstanding contribution to fast, comfortable train travel. The Class "H" enables North Western passenger trains to maintain an even speed uphill and downhill . . . it eliminates jerky starts and stops . . . *it assures a smooth-running train at all times.*

CHICAGO & NORTH WESTERN RY.

and converted it to a mechanical refrigerator car. The car could be set to maintain automatically any temperature down to 15 degrees below zero.

Although the Northern Pacific was often considered the potato railroad because of its famous and delicious baked potato dinners served in the dining cars, potato traffic was also an important traffic item for the C&NW. (New England's Bangor & Aroostook was also considered a "Potato Railroad.") The C&NW transformed and improved its potato-handling yard near downtown Chicago in 1957.

Wood Street Terminal was the central market area for potatoes and onions. The C&NW built a new office building and additional trackage, and improved communications for the potato brokers who could now conduct their business transactions right at the improved and expanded facility.

The C&NW once handled over 19,000 carloads of produce annually of which potatoes accounted for more than 17,000 cars. The facil-

ity covered about 60 acres with trackage for 550 cars. Additional trackage provided space for over 1800 additional cars for holding, inspection, or reconsignment. The C&NW switched the yard six nights per week setting in new loads. From about 8 a.m. to after 10 a.m. each day, the dealers met, showed, inspected, bought and sold carloads of produce at a provided shelter. The remainder of the day was devoted to loading and unloading the purchases.

The yard was originally built in 1930. Part of the innovations in 1957 included both day and night switching crews at the Wood Street Terminal for the classification and movement of cars consigned to this point. Part of the facility included covered unloading platforms with 34-foot-long automatic scales for weighing truckloads of potatoes. Lights enabled crews to switch, mark, and inspect both equipment and the various types of loads all night long thereby creating a very effective service system.

This publicity photo on the Overland Route shows an example of the artistic bridge structures on the C&NW. (C&NW Photo)

One very interesting facet of C&NW services took place in 1958. A foreign trade guide book was published by the foreign freight department. It was originally designed for the C&NW traffic department, but the booklet suddenly became known and was in high demand by Midwestern shippers. The handbook contained such topics as explanations of common terminology and examples of certain forms used for exporting goods, clearing customs, detailed regulations, and procedures for both export and import shipments and maps. There were also detailed descriptions of the various lake ports served by the railroad, among them Chicago, Milwaukee, Green Bay, Duluth, and Superior.

The foreign trade book was part of a series of publications issued by the C&NW to provide assistance for the marketing staff (once called the Traffic Department).

Other C&NW publications included a pulpwood marketing handbook issued by the Resources Development department. Still other topics included:

- The Bentonite clay deposits in South Dakota and Wyoming
- Development of South Dakota agriculture by participation in the development of irrigation
- The Black Hills timber industry, including descriptions of existing sawmills and wood products industries throughout the area.

This type of marketing research led to more innovations. One example was the "multiple-car" freight rate, which was originally established to promote the South Dakota pulpwood industry. The C&NW negotiated with various mill operators and a multiple-car rate based on 25-carload minimums was established. The first pulpwood shipment out of Deadwood, South Dakota, took place in October 1958.

One of the most advanced innovations devised by the C&NW during the late 1950s was "CAR-FAX." This new system was able to keep tabs on freight car and train movements as they occurred 24 hours a day. At 68 reporting points along the railroad's 9300-mile system, waybill and car reporting information was placed on punched cards—this at a time when computer systems to handle such complex operations as freight car and train movements were in their infancy.

Among the benefits of CAR-FAX were:
1. Fast and accurate car-tracing services through CAR-FAX headquarters in Chicago and all of the C&NW's traffic offices.
2. Fast and accurate reconsignments or diversions of freight en route.
3. Immediate information on delayed shipments.
4. Improved car utilization.
5. Reduced switching time through advanced train consists, which in turn allowed for advance planning for switching at all yards.

The program provided the ability to prepare a variety of reports for traffic, operations, and accounting from one source. The system provided information which enabled the traffic department to analyze traffic trends and evaluate sales efforts for better customer service. The operating department had new levels of information for car uti-

lization and a more effective system for car movement. The accounting department received faster information for freight revenues as well as car per diem statistics.

Specific reports available with the North Western's new CAR-FAX system included:

Loading summaries
Loading summaries by commodity
Commodity loading analysis
Unearned revenues
New loading reports
Loading summaries by state
Equipment loading summaries
Empty car locations
Summaries of cars on line
Empty car forwarding
Cars to and from connecting railroads
Per diem distribution by division
Car tracing and per diem records
Car movement reporting
Bad-order reports

C&NW subsidiaries wore the C&NW image, but carried their own company initials or reporting marks. Note the "CStPM&O" for the Omaha Road—the Chicago, St. Paul, Minneapolis & Omaha—beneath the number 602 on this very powerful 4-6-2 at St. Paul, Minnesota, in May 1948. (Harold K. Vollrath Collection)

One of the railroads purchased and folded into the C&NW was the Minneapolis & St. Louis. This ex-M&StL GP9 wore a typical example of the yellow-and-green C&NW scheme—but note the M&StL initials below the cab insignia on No. 709, which was photographed during switching operations at the Cedar Lake Yard in Minneapolis in 1971. (Author)

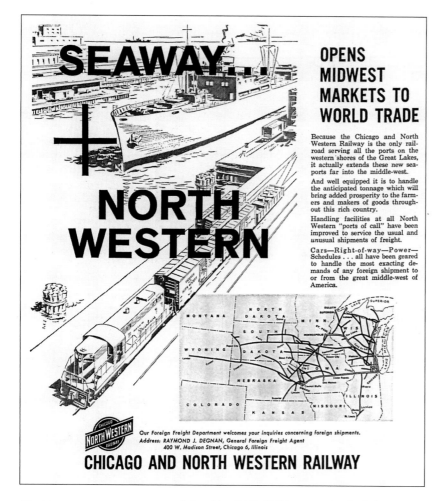

World commerce came to the C&NW's doorstep in the late 1950s with the opening of the St. Lawrence Seaway. (Author's Collection)

Monthly CAR-FAX reports included:
• Regional traffic summaries
• Agency commodity reports
• Agency firm summaries
• Shipper and consignee analysis
• Controlled firm summaries
• Gateway reports
• Empty cars on line
• Car detentions
• Hire of freight equipment.

The operating concepts of CAR-FAX were studied by other railroads, which in turn led to more developments on freight car scheduling and reporting—the Missouri Pacific's car reporting system is but one example.

The North Western's CAR-FAX system provided an incredible new knowledge of the railroad's operations and service for and with shippers. It launched the C&NW into a new era of operations in the 1960s.

Dieselization was complete and a series of new trends would change the configuration of the company in many ways, which included new concepts in intermodal traffic, abandonment of many secondary main lines and branch lines, a series of railroad acquisitions, and eventual merger into the Union Pacific.

Before getting too far ahead into the 1960s and beyond, we have to back track to 1957 when the C&NW began a series of changes throughout the system.

During the spring of 1957, a new freight car shop was completed at Clinton, Iowa. The new shop replaced 14 shops around the system and was expected to pay for itself within three years.

The summer of 1957 saw the opening of a new pink quartzite quarry in central Wisconsin, which provided high-grade ballast for the company and lent North Western tracks a pinkish hue.

Dieselization was completed in 1957 through an improved motive-power scheduling system. The new system provided the company the ability to handle additional trains with fewer locomotives.

Proviso Yard was studied carefully, and improved scheduling provided the opportunity for part of the terminal to be closed. This in turn provided an opportunity for 74 acres to be used for industrial development. The world's largest

An interesting scene on the former Chicago Great Western is this meet at Mc Intire, Iowa, (north of Oelwein). A northbound C&NW freight is running on the main line, at right, while the southbound local (with one car) has backed onto the Rochester Branch to clear the main on June 28, 1972. The CGW was known for its "lashups" of five, six, or more F-units on freight trains. (William S. Kuba)

top: The evolution of the yellow-and-green paint schemes. Alco RSD-4 No. 1516—at Des Plaines, Illinois, on May 25, 1958—illustrates the full end stripes, as well as the "Route of the Streamliners" slogan ("Route of the 400" was on the opposite side.) (Fred Ziebe, Author's Collection)

second from top: The next phase had one full stripe on the ends, but no passenger train slogans. (Author)

lower left: S-2 No. 1267, at Chicago in January 1966, in the final scheme—no end stripes. (Fred Ziebe)

lower right: Alco C-425s Nos. 402 and 401. (John H. Kuehl)

bottom left: Some units, like SW1200 No. 1218, had split yellow and green cabs instead of solid green. (Author)

bottom right: SD45 No. 6512 in 1988. (Thomas A. Dorin)

freight yard could no longer boast of such an achievement. These innovations were only a small part of the programs undertaking during the mid- to late 1950s to improve the financial condition of the railroad.

One of the interesting aspects of the C&NW was not only the abandonment of several branch lines and secondary main lines throughout the area, but the purchase of still other railroad lines which in turn were merged into the system. One of the primary purposes for the various railroad company purchases was the creation of "through-line" services. One of the first purchases was the Litchfield & Madison in southern Illinois.

The L&M connected with the C&NW at Benld, Illinois. The railroad was 44 miles long between Litchfield to Madison and East St. Louis, Illinois. The C&NW-L&M interchange business amounted to 43 percent of the L&M's traffic. The company owned but four locomotives and 297 hopper cars in 1957. The stockholders approved the merger in October 1957, which was also subject to the Interstate Commerce Commission's approval. The merger date was January 2, 1958.

One other thought for expansion took place during the mid-1950s. The C&NW pondered the idea of building a 185-mile extension of their

railroad from Lander, Wyoming, to Ogden, Utah. At the time, the extension would have given the North Western a direct connection with the Southern Pacific and Western Pacific railroads. The idea was discarded, and as we now know, the C&NW, SP and WP as well as the Missouri Pacific lines are now all part of the Union Pacific.

The next merger step by the C&NW was the purchase of the Minneapolis & St. Louis Railway in November 1960. At the time, the C&NW System was about 9,300 miles. The inclusion of the M&StL created a new 10,700-mile system. The primary routes of the M&StL extended from the Twin Cities to Aberdeen, South Dakota, as well as two routes southward to Des Moines and Oskaloosa (where to the two routes joined) and continued to Peoria, Illinois.

Former Minneapolis & St. Louis motive power and rolling stock took on the C&NW color scheme, but retained the M&StL initials on motive power as well as M&StL reporting marks on freight equipment. Remarkably, former M&StL cars with M&StL reporting marks and a C&NW herald could still be seen, on rare occasions, as late as 2001.

The next major merger for the C&NW was the purchase of the Chicago Great Western on July 1, 1968. As had been the case with the M&StL, the CGW equipment was painted in the C&NW schemes but retained CGW initials and/or reporting marks.

Less than a month later—on July 29, 1968, to be exact—the C&NW acquired the Des Moines & Central Iowa Railway, which in turn owned the majority of the Fort Dodge, Des Moines & Southern Railway.

Within the next month, the C&NW and the Missouri Pacific jointly purchased the Alton & Southern Railroad. The A&S's name was changed to the Alton & Southern Railway.

At the end of 1970, the C&NW consisted of 11,046 miles. The company had been involved in possible merger plans with the Rock Island and eventually the Milwaukee Road. However, neither of these plans made any progress.

During its final 25 years of independent operation, the C&NW abandoned substantial segments of a wide variety of rail lines throughout the Midwest. Some routes were sold to new operators like the Dakota, Minnesota & Eastern. The rail routes to places such as Ashland, Wisconsin, and Duluth-Superior were gone. For continued access to the Twin Ports, the C&NW obtained trackage rights over the Wisconsin Central from Superior to Central Wisconsin where it joined the North

lower right: Work trains are an important facet of a railroad's operations. In the spring of 1952 Work Extra 1536 West stops by Shorewood, Wisconsin, with a Jordan spreader, a tool car, and a wooden bay window caboose still in the red livery. (Jim Scribbins)

below: Jim Scribbins captured a classic meet as train 488 arrives at Butler Yard (Milwaukee) with a mix of intermodal and regular freight as Geep No. 1559 waits for clearance to switch the rear-end of the time freight before it continues its journey to Proviso Yard, just west of Chicago.

Western main line from the Twin Cities to Chicago. The company obtained trackage rights over the Burlington Northern between Superior and the Twin Cities.

Acquisitions of trackage also took place. The C&NW obtained the Rock Island's "Spine Line" between the Twin Cities and Kansas City. By 1990, the C&NW's route mileage had dropped to approximately 4,800 miles, not including trackage rights. Meanwhile, the Union Pacific began looking at the C&NW to augment its system to and from Chicago and the Twin Cities. The merger took place in 1995. The new Union Pacific System consisted of not only the original UP and the C&NW, but also the Missouri Pacific, Cotton Belt, the Rio Grande, Southern Pacific and the Western Pacific. Repainted C&NW freight equipment now carries C&NW reporting marks, but with a Union Pacific insignia (see Chapter 9).

The C&NW was one incredible railroad. The remaining chapters look at the freight services provided by the company from the postwar era through to the 1990s.

Cabooses played a major safety role for many decades on North America's railroads. This C&NW photo illustrates the interior of a wooden caboose with its bunks, desks, heater, and other equipment.

The bay window area of a later steel caboose, built by Thrall Car for the C&NW, was quite a bit more spartan in its interior arrangements, and lacked the "rustic" charm of the wooden cars. (Both, Author's Collection)

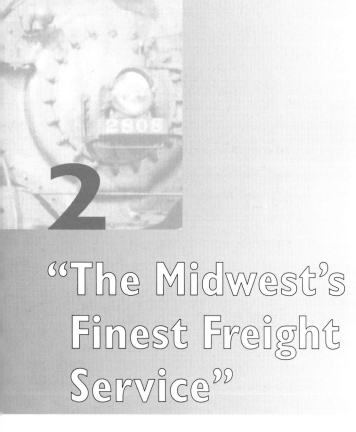

2

"The Midwest's Finest Freight Service"

The advertisement on the passenger timetables said it all. The C&NW provided an extraordinary freight service throughout its 9,000-mile-plus system in the years following World War II and the Korean War. What made the C&NW and the Omaha Road unique was the combination of extensive main lines and the numerous branch lines throughout Chicago & North Western territory from Chicago to Michigan and west to South Dakota and Wyoming. Let's take a look at some of the wide variety of C&NW freight services and train operations during the postwar period.

The C&NW, as did almost all other railroads in North America, offered an extensive Less than Carload (LCL) service throughout its system for many decades. For the most part, the railroad hired various local trucking companies to provide pick-up and delivery service for the LCL traffic.

However, this type of arrangement had a low quality level. The C&NW tried an experiment in 1947 with lease arrangements with a truck rental firm for handling pick-up and delivery in Milwaukee. With the lease arrangement, the pick-up and delivery service was under the railroad's full control, and the quality level skyrocketed. The company expanded the idea to a major operation in Chicago as well as Waukegan, Omaha, Des Moines, Eau Claire, Madison, and Mankato.

The Chicago operation involved the lease of 50 trailers and 25 tractors from Motor Express, Inc., a Chicago-area leasing company. Although the drivers were on the lessor's payroll, they were assigned exclusively to the C&NW fleet. The lease arrangement provided a new level of flexibility for dispatching the service, which in turn provided a better flow at the freight houses. The C&NW's objective was to be able to forward all freight the

same evening if a pick-up had been requested by 2 p.m., and to deliver all freight on the morning of arrival. This type of lease arrangement was expanded to many stations throughout the system by 1950.

Sadly enough, the C&NW decided to drop all pick-up and delivery service in 1957. As one could guess, this was met with a great deal of opposition, but eventually the ICC permitted the operation to be phased out.

Refrigerator cars played a major role for perishable traffic on the C&NW. During the late summer, one could find strings of refrigerator cars on the line north of Antigo, in anticipation of the potato harvest in that area of Wisconsin.

The paper industry was a major source of freight revenue for the C&NW. The lines from northern Michigan, Ashland, and Superior were arteries for much of the paper industry. This

The C&NW's 2-8-4 Berkshires were exceptionally handsome locomotives and very effective freight haulers. Originally serving in coal train and time freight service, part of the Berkshire fleet went north to the ore lines when dieselization began on the Overland Route and the southern Illinois coal line. (Paul Stringham, Rail Photo Service; Author's Collection)

right: It is June 9, 1956, and steam is still part of the C&NW's freight motive power picture. Omaha Road 2-8-2 No. 417 heads up a southbound local just north of Humbird, Wis., on the Twin Cities– Milwaukee main line. Humbird is located just north of Merrillan between Wyeville and Eau Claire. (Jim Scribbins)

below: A northbound local freight powered by No. 421, an Omaha 2-8-2, rolls along between Elroy and Hustler, Wis., on the Twin Cities main line, also on June 9, 1956. Close to the end of the steam era, the Omaha powered a number of its wayfreights with 2-8-2s which had been bumped from time freights by new diesel power. (Jim Scribbins)

included the movement of pulpwood logs to the mills, and the outbound finished paper products. Cities such as Ashland, Wausau, Wisconsin Rapids, Green Bay, and the Fox River Valley had many paper mills. The C&NW's share of this traffic included gondolas loaded with pulp logs and box cars for the finished paper.

Still another major source of revenue for the C&NW was grain traffic. The company served the grain country from eastern Minnesota to western South Dakota with their main line and dozens of branch lines throughout those states as well as Iowa and Nebraska. For most of the history of the C&NW, the grain was handled in box cars with grain doors. Moving into mid-1960s and beyond to the 1990s and the UP merger, the grain was moved in the 100-ton capacity covered hopper cars. Most of the grain moved eastward to the Twin Cities, the Milwaukee/Chicago area, and Duluth-Superior. In fact, the C&NW built a grain elevator at Superior, which has been a primary source of traffic for the company. This is still true today with the Union Pacific.

As a side note, when the initial plans were made regarding this elevator, there was some thought given to the idea of building the elevator in Washburn, Wisconsin. Had that been the case,

Ten-Wheelers (4-6-0 wheel arrangement) also played a role in the C&NW's local freight train operations. No. 1402 is arriving at Plymouth, Wisconsin, with such a freight train in 1938. (J. J. Campbell, Author's Collection)

above: With 2-8-2 No. 2458 for power, a time freight makes its way over Radnor Hill on the southern Illinois line. The train is moving slow and the engine is working hard, providing "stack music" which signified the success of moving freight during the 1940s. (William S. Kuba Collection)

right: Radnor Hill, near Peoria, was an operating headache requiring double-heading and sometimes even triple-heading of locomotives. Nos. 2802 and 2582 charge the hill in grand fashion on July 25, 1943. (James Bowie, William S. Kuba Collection)

bottom: C&NW No. 2811, Class J-4, is taking a train under the South Adams Street viaduct in Peoria on July 3, 1947. (Paul Stringham, Author's Collection)

left: No. 1803, a 2-8-0, is handling an east-bound local freight with 18 cars at Chadron, Nebraska. Running as Extra 1803 East, the train has a mixture of freight cars including stock cars for serving the beef cattle market. (Charles Ost, William S. Kuba Collection)

middle: Extra 2575 West steams up-grade through West Allis, Wis., with a long string of empty stock cars during March 1947. (Jim Scribbins)

below: Shifting a bit to the west at Mankato, Minnesota, a west-bound train curves into the yard in 1948. The east-west C&NW main line from Chicago to Rapid City crossed the Omaha Road's north-south main line from Minneapolis-St. Paul to Omaha here. (Charles Ost, William S. Kuba Collection)

right: The interchange of freight in Chicago was time-consuming and complicated, requiring many "transfer runs" between yards of the various railroads. In this photo, C&NW Class J Mikado No. 2487 is arriving at the Belt Railway of Chicago's Clearing Yard in 1938 with a freight transfer from Proviso Yard. (H. W. Pontin, Author's Collection)

bottom: By late 1954, the only mainline steam on the Iowa Division was to be found on the local freights. No. 1221, a 4-6-0, appears at Belle Plaine, Iowa, on November 11, 1954, as F3 diesel No. 4057A rolls mainline tonnage east. No. 1221 worked six-day weeks, three days on a Cedar Rapids–Belle Plaine local and three days between Cedar Rapids and Tipton, Iowa. (William S. Kuba)

the former Omaha line between the Twin Cities and Ashland-Washburn-Bayfield would probably still be in existence. (The same may have also been true regarding the ex-Northern Pacific line between Superior and Ashland.)

The fleet of freight trains remained relatively stable between the 1940s and the 1960s. In fact, there was very few changes made in freight train numbers. One subtle change was the elimination of various freight train names, which took place during the early 1940s.

A few examples of freight train names included No. 84, the *Hawkeye*, eastward out of Sioux Falls on the Omaha Road; No. 169, the *Frolake*, on the Ashland Division through Eland; No. 281, the *Forester*, to Ashland, Wisconsin; No. 282, the *Ojibwa*, from Ashland; No. 170, the *Tolake* on the Ashland Division through Eland; and No. 174, *Stock Freight*, a Wednesday-only freight between Eland and Marshfield on the Ashland Division. There were many other name freights throughout the C&NW system during the 1930s but by the 1940s the names were disappearing fast.

Alpha-lettering train symbols replaced freight train numbers during the final 15 years or so of the C&NW's corporate existence prior to the 1995 UP merger. The table on page 25 lists

(continued on page 25)

No. 2642 was a powerful 0-8-0 steam switch engine ideal for handling transfer runs, as shown here with such an assignment in the Chicago Terminals. (H. W. Pontin, Author's Collection)

The North Western published condensed freight schedules, such as the June 1960 edition (above) and also promoted "The Midwest's Finest Freight Service" on the covers of passenger timetables. The October 26, 1958, public timetable featured the road's "400" streamliners on one side of the cover, and this artwork on the other side. (Both, Author's Collection)

right: Two F7A units in the green-yellow-and-black color scheme power Extra 4099C West with 91 cars on the main line west of Butler, Wisconsin, in the fall of 1950. (Jim Scribbins)

Chicago-Milwaukee-St. Paul-Minneapolis-Superior-Duluth — TABLE 3

Northbound—Read Down   Southbound—Read Up

491 Daily Ex. Sun. and Mon.	471 ⊙	477	483-171	Stations	172-490 □	488	472 ⊙	492 Daily Ex. Sun. and Mon.
....	9:00 PM Mo.	4:15 PM Mo.	7:00 AM Mo.	Lv.Chicago (Proviso) Ar.	11:59 PM Mo.	11:00 AM Tu.	....	....
2:00 AM Tu.	....	....	....	Lv. Chicago (40th St.) Ar.	....	....	11:30 AM Tu.	2:30 PM Tu.
5:00 AM Tu.	....	7:30 PM Mo.	10:30 AM Mo.	Ar.Milwaukee(Butler)Ar.	8:00 PM Mo.	7:00 AM Tu.	....	11:00 AM Tu.
8:45 AM Tu.	....	11:00 PM Mo.	4:30 PM Mo.	Ar......Adams......(Lv.	4:00 PM Mo.	2:15 PM Tu.	....	7:45 AM Tu.
11:30 AM Tu.	8:00 AM Tu.	2:00 AM Tu.	9:30 PM Mo.	Ar....Altoona....{Lv.	1:00 PM Mo.	11:15 PM Mo.	10:00 PM Mo.	4:50 AM Tu.
				Ar.	12:30 PM Mo.	10:45 PM Mo.	7:00 PM Mo.	4:00 AM Tu.
2:00 PM Tu.	....	7:00 AM Tu.	10:30 PM Mo.	Ar.....Eau Claire....Lv.	11:00 AM Mo.	10:00 PM Mo.	....	6:00 AM Tu.
2:30 PM Tu.	1:00 PM Tu.	5:00 AM Tu.	12:30 AM Tu.	Ar...East St.Paul...Lv.	10:00 AM Mo.	8:00 PM Mo.	4:00 PM Mo.	2:00 AM Tu.
			1:30 AM Tu.	Ar.. Minn. Transfer .Lv.				
3:15 PM Tu.	2:00 PM Tu.	6:00 AM Tu.	2:30 AM Tu.	Ar..E. Minneapolis..Lv.	9:30 AM Mo.	6:30 PM Mo.	3:00 PM Mo.	12:01 AM Tu.
			171		**172**			
....	....	....	5:15 AM Tu.	Lv.....Altoona....Ar.	8:00 AM Mo.	....		
....	....	....	9:10 AM Tu.	Ar.....Spooner....Ar.	4:30 AM Mo.			
....	....	....	1:30 PM Tu.	Ar.....Superior....Ar.	3:00 AM Mo.			
....	....	....	3:30 PM Tu.	Ar.....Duluth.....Lv.	2:00 AM Mo.			

Note: These schedules are planned to provide fast through connections with all carriers from and to Eastern Points

⊙ Nos. 471 and 472 operates via Janesville and Madison.
No. 471 arrives Madison 3:00 AM. No. 472 arrives Madison 6:00 AM.
Note: Schedules are coordinated with connecting lines at St. Paul-Minneapolis and Duluth to effect fast through service to and from Pacific Coast, Canadian and Intermediate points.

□ Cars moved via 40th St. (Chicago) connect with No. 472 from Altoona.

CHICAGO - PEORIA - ST. LOUIS — TABLE 4

Southbound—Read Down   Northbound—Read Up

Note: These schedules are coordinated with C&NW trains to provide fast through service from and to the West and North.

381-385	381	383	Stations	380	386	384-254	
11:00 AM Mo.	11:00 AM Mo.	9:30 PM Mo.	Lv.....Chicago (Proviso).....Ar.	4:30 PM Mo.	5:30 AM Tu.	11:30 AM Mo.	....
2:00 PM Mo.	2:00 PM Mo.	1:00 AM Tu.	Ar.........Nelson.........Ar.	1:00 PM Mo.	11:45 PM Mo.	6:00 AM Mo.	
1:00 AM Tu.			Ar.........Peoria.........Lv.			2:00 AM Mo.	
....	6:30 PM Mo.	4:45 AM Tu.	Ar........South Pekin.....Ar.	8:00 AM Mo.	6:15 PM Mo.		
....	10:00 PM Mo.	9:00 AM Tu.	Ar.........Benld.........Lv.	5:30 AM Mo.	3:15 PM Mo.		
....	11:30 PM Mo.	11:30 AM Tu.	Ar.........E.St.Louis......Lv.	2:30 AM Mo.	12:30 PM Mo.		

Note: Schedules are planned to provide fast through connections with all carriers to and from the South and Southwest.

CHICAGO - DES MOINES — TABLE 5

Westbound—Read Down   Eastbound—Read Up

Note: All schedules are coordinated with C&NW trains operated between Chicago and Wisconsin, Minnesota and Upper Michigan points to provide fast through service.

123	Stations	124
3:00 AM Tu.	Lv..Chicago (Proviso).Ar.	3:00 PM Tu.
6:00 AM Tu.	Ar.....Nelson......Ar.	10:00 AM Tu.
8:00 AM Tu.	Ar....Clinton.....Lv.	9:00 AM Tu.
10:00 AM Tu.	Lv....Clinton.....Ar.	5:30 AM Tu.
12:01 PM Tu.	Ar.. Cedar Rapids ..Ar.	2:00 AM Tu.
2:00 PM Tu.	Ar...Belle Plaine..Ar.	1:30 AM Tu.
3:00 PM Tu.	Ar.. Marshalltown ..Ar.	12:30 AM Tu.
4:00 PM Tu.	Ar......Ames.....Lv.	11:00 PM Mo.
4:30 PM Tu.	Lv......Ames.....Ar.	10:30 PM Mo.
7:00 PM Tu.	Ar...Des Moines...Lv.	8:45 PM Mo.

Note: These schedules are planned to provide fast through connections with all carriers for traffic destined to and received from the Southwest and South Pacific Coast Points.

CHICAGO - ASHLAND — TABLE 6

Northbound—Read Down   Southbound—Read Up

295-281	Stations	282-296 Ex. Sun.
295 Daily		
8:15 PM Mo.	Lv..Chicago (Proviso).Ar.	4:45 AM We.
....	Ar. Milwaukee (Butler) Ar.	11:55 PM Tu.
2:50 AM Tu.	Ar. North Fond du Lac. Lv.	7:00 PM Tu.
281 Dly. Ex. Sun.		
10:00 AM Tu.	Lv. North Fond du Lac. Ar.	4:00 AM Tu.
11:00 AM Tu.	Ar.....Oshkosh.....Ar.	2:00 AM Tu.
11:59 AM Tu.	Ar....New London...Ar.	9:04 PM Mo.
12:20 PM Tu.	Ar.....Clintonville....Ar.	8:27 PM Mo.
3:00 PM Tu.	Ar......Eland......Ar.	4:00 PM Mo.
4:30 PM Tu.	Ar.....Antigo.....Lv.	3:15 PM Mo.
7:00 PM Tu.	Lv.....Antigo.....Ar.	2:45 PM Mo.
8:30 PM Tu.	Ar...Rhinelander..Ar.	12:01 PM Mo.
9:40 PM Tu.	Ar.....Hurley.....Lv.	8:00 AM Mo.
7:00 AM We.	Ar.....Ironwood....Lv.	7:55 AM Mo.
5:00 AM We.	Ar.....Ashland....Lv.	7:00 AM Mo.

GREEN BAY - IRON MOUNTAIN — TABLE 7

Northbound—Read Down   Southbound—Read Up

37 Dly. Ex. Sat.	Stations	36 Dly. Ex. Sun.
2:00 PM Mo.	Lv...North Green Bay..Ar.	3:00 PM Mo.
6:00 AM Mo.	Ar....Iron Mountain..Ar.	9:10 AM Mo.
6:30 AM Tu.	Ar.......Antoine.....Lv.	8:00 AM Mo.

DULUTH - MINNEAPOLIS - OMAHA — TABLE 8

Southbound—Read Down   Northbound—Read Up

Note: These schedules are planned to provide fast through connections at Duluth and the Twin Cities with all carriers from and to Pacific Coast, Canadian and intermediate points.

74	17	Stations	20	73
11:00 PM Mo.	......	Lv.....Duluth....Ar.	......	9:00 PM Tu.
11:30 PM Mo.	......	Lv......Superior....Ar.	......	6:00 PM Tu.
3:30 AM Tu.	......	Ar......Spooner....Lv.	......	1:00 PM Tu.
5:55 AM Tu.	......	Lv......Spooner....Ar.	......	11:50 AM Tu.
76 Ex. Sun.				**75 Ex. Sun.**
5:30 PM Mo.	......	Lv.....Ashland....Ar.	......	6:00 AM We.
9:30 PM Mo.	......	Ar.....Spooner....Lv.	......	2:25 AM We.
				174 Daily
9:00 AM Tu.	......	Ar. West Minneapolis Lv.	......	6:30 AM Tu.
......	11:59 PM Tu.	Lv. West Minneapolis Ar.	3:30 AM Tu.	......
......	4:00 AM We.	Ar.....Mankato....Ar.	10:15 PM Mo.	......
......	12:01 PM We.	Ar.....Sioux City...Lv.	3:00 PM Mo.	......
......	1:30 PM We.	Lv...Sioux City....Ar.	1:30 PM Mo.	......
......	5:00 PM We.	Ar.....Omaha....Lv.	10:00 AM Mo.	......

Note: These schedules are planned to effect fast through connections at Omaha with all carriers for traffic destined to and received from Western and Southwestern points.

CHICAGO - CHADRON - CASPER - RAPID CITY — TABLE 9

Westbound—Read Down   Eastbound—Read Up

	261-117-619-617	Stations	256-618-620-252	
......	**261**		**252**	......
	6:30 PM Mo.	Lv.Chicago (Proviso) Ar.	9:00 PM Th.	
	2:30 PM Tu.	Ar..Missouri Valley. Ar.	6:15 AM Th.	
......	**117**		**256 Ex. Mon.**	......
	10:30 PM Tu.	Lv..Missouri Valley. Ar.	8:30 PM We.	
	2:25 AM We.	Ar.....Norfolk....Ar.	3:00 PM We.	
......	**Ex. Mon.**			......
	5:05 PM We.	Ar.....Chadron....Lv.	2:30 AM We.	
......	**619 Ex. Sun.**		**620 Ex. Sun.**	......
	6:30 AM Th.	Ar......Casper....Lv.	7:30 AM Tu.	
......	**617 Tu. Th. Sa.**		**618 Mo. We. Fr.**	......
	3:00 PM Th.	Ar......Lander....Lv.	9:45 AM Mo.	
......	**117**		**256 Ex. Sun.**	......
	8:05 AM Th.	Ar...Rapid City...Lv.	6:45 PM Tu.	
	10:45 AM Th.	Ar..Belle Fourche..Lv.	4:30 PM Tu.	

Condensed schedules like these from 1960 (continued on the following two pages) gave C&NW shippers a snapshot of the freight service they could expect. (Author's Collection)

CHICAGO - MILWAUKEE - GREEN BAY - ISHPEMING - IRON MOUNTAIN

Northbound—Read Down / Southbound—Read Up — **TABLE 10**

297 Dly. Ex. Mon.	173 Dly. Ex. Mon.	187-39	295	Station	180	296	172 Dly. Ex. Mon.	290 Dly. Ex. Mon.
....Lv....	....Lv.	10:00 PM Mo.	8:15 PM Mo.	Lv..Chicago (Proviso).Ar.	6:00 AM We.	4:45 AM Tu.		
6:00 PM Tu.	2:00 PM Tu.	1:45 AM Tu.	11:30 PM Mo.	Ar....Milwaukee....Ar.		11:55 PM Mo.	1:30 PM Tu.	4:00 PM Tu.
				Ar.Milwaukee(Butler)Ar.	12:10 AM We.			
	3:50 PM Tu.	4:30 AM Tu.		Ar....Sheboygan....Ar.	9:45 PM Tu.		8:45 AM Tu.	
	6:00 PM Tu.	5:40 AM Tu.		Ar....Manitowoc....Ar.	7:45 PM Tu.		7:20 AM Tu.	
		231 Dly. Ex. Sat. & Sun.			**204** Dly. Ex. Sat. & Sun.			
		9:00 AM Tu.		Ar....Two Rivers....Lv.	5:15 PM Tu.			
	7:30 PM Tu.	8:30 AM Tu.		Ar...No. Green Bay..Lv.	6:30 PM Tu.			
		2:00 PM Tu.		Lv...No. Green Bay..Ar.	3:20 PM Tu.		6:10 AM Tu.	
		2:50 PM Tu.		Ar....Marinette....Ar.	11:40 AM Tu.			
		3:20 PM Tu.		Ar....Menominee....Ar.	11:35 AM Tu.			
		9:30 PM Tu.		Ar....Escanaba....Ar.	6:45 PM Mo.			
		2:30 AM We.		Ar....Negaunee....Ar.	3:30 PM Mo.			
		5:00 AM We.		Ar....Ishpeming....Ar.	3:00 PM Mo.			
		35 Dly. Ex. Sun.			**36**			
		6:00 AM We.		Ar...Iron Mountain..Lv.	9:00 AM Tu.			
1:50 AM We.			2:50 AM Tu.	Ar.North Fond du Lac.Lv.		7:00 PM Mo.		11:00 AM Tu.
9:00 AM We.			2:50 AM Tu.	Lv.North Fond du Lac.Ar.		5:45 PM Mo.		10:00 AM Tu.
10:00 AM We.			3:21 AM Tu.	Ar....Oshkosh....Ar.		5:20 PM Mo.		6:00 AM Tu.
11:00 AM We.			4:25 AM Tu.	Ar. Neenah-Menasha Ar.		5:00 PM Mo.		4:00 AM Tu.
11:30 AM We.			5:00 AM Tu.	Ar....Appleton....Ar.		4:30 PM Mo.		3:00 AM Tu.
2:00 PM We.			7:00 AM Tu.	Ar...No. Green Bay..Lv.		1:25 PM Mo.		2:00 AM Tu.

Chicago - Mason City - Huron / Watertown - Sioux Falls

Westbound—Read Down / Eastbound—Read Up — **TABLE 11**

261-125-495-21-85	Station	84-20-126-256
6:30 P M Mo.	Lv. Chicago (Proviso)..Ar.	11:45 AM Tu.
1:00 AM Tu.	Ar.......Clinton.......Lv.	....
2:00 AM Tu.	Lv.......Clinton.......Ar.	....
6:00 AM Tu.	Ar....Belle Plaine....Lv.	4:30 AM Tu.
125 Dly. Ex. Sun.		**126** Dly. Ex. Sun.
9:00 A M Tu.	Lv....Belle Plaine....Ar.	3:00 A M Tu.
12:30 P M Tu.	Ar....Mason City....Lv.	11:45 P M Mo.
7:15 P M Tu.	Lv....Mason City....Ar.	11:15 P M Mo.
10:30 P M Tu.	Ar.......Butterfield......Ar.	8:30 P M Mo.
12:30 A M We.	Ar.........Tracy.........Ar.	6:45 P M Mo.
495 Dly. Ex. Sun.		
8:30 P M We.	Ar........Huron........Lv.	4:00 P M Mo.
21 Ex. Sa. & Su.		**20** Dly. Ex. Sun.
12:30 A M Fr.	Ar....Watertown....Lv.	4:10 P M Mo.
85 Dly. Ex. Sun.		**84** Dly. Ex. Sun.
8:00 A M We.	Ar.....Sioux Falls....Lv.	6:05 P M Mo.

CHICAGO - ROCKFORD - FREEPORT

Northbound—Read Down / Southbound—Read Up — **TABLE 12**

261-95 Ex. Sat.	Station	94-386 Ex. Sun.
6:30 P M Mo.	Lv..Chicago (Proviso).Ar.	5:30 AM Tu.
8:00 P M Mo.	Ar....West Chicago...Ar.	9:45 P M Mo.
12:30 A M Tu.	Ar........Elgin........Ar.	9:00 P M Mo.
2:05 A M Tu.	Ar.....Belvidere.....Ar.	7:20 P M Mo.
3:05 A M Tu.	Ar......Rockford......Ar.	6:15 P M Mo.
5:30 A M Tu.	Ar......Freeport.....Lv.	4:45 P M Mo.

CHICAGO - WAUKEGAN - MILWAUKEE

Northbound—Read Down / Southbound—Read Up — **TABLE 13**

289 Dly. Ex. Sun.	285	Station	280	290 Dly. Ex. Sun.
1:00 AM Mo.	7:30 PM Mo.	Lv..Chicago (Proviso).Ar.	11:35 P M Mo.	
		Lv..Chicago (40th St.).Ar.		2:30 AM Tu.
	10:15 PM Mo.	Ar.....Waukegan....Ar.	9:30 P M Mo.	12:30 AM Tu.
	10:50 PM Mo.	Ar.....Kenosha....Ar.	8:55 P M Mo.	11:30 PM Mo.
	11:35 PM Mo.	Ar......Racine......Ar.	8:20 P M Mo.	10:30 PM Mo.
	12:25 AM Tu.	Ar....Carrollville....Ar.		
	12:45 AM Tu.	Ar......Cudahy......Ar.	7:45 P M Mo.	9:30 PM Mo.
5:00 AM Mo.	....	Ar.....Milwaukee....Lv.	7:15 P M Mo.	8:00 PM Mo.
3:30 AM Tu.		Ar. Milwaukee (Butler)		

MILWAUKEE - WINONA - MANKATO - HURON - RAPID CITY

Westbound—Read Down / Eastbound—Read Up — **TABLE 14**

495	Station	482
10:20 PM Mo.	Lv.Milwaukee (Butler)Ar.	8:30 PM Th.
2:35 AM Tu.	Ar........Adams........Ar.	12:30 PM Th.
2:10 AM Tu.	Ar........Winona........Ar.	6:40 AM Th.
8:15 PM Tu.	Ar.....Rochester....Ar.	4:00 AM Th.
11:00 PM Tu.	Ar.......Waseca.......Ar.	7:20 PM We.
5:15 PM We.	Ar.......Mankato.......Ar.	6:00 PM We.
10:00 AM We.	Ar.........Tracy.........Lv.	2:15 PM We.
Ex. Sun.		**126** Ex. Sun.
3:30 PM We.	Lv.........Tracy.........Ar.	9:00 PM Tu.
8:30 PM We.	Ar.........Huron.........Ar.	4:00 PM Tu.
		62 Ex. Sun.
7:40 AM Th.	Lv.........Huron.........Ar.	11:25 AM Tu.
1:25 PM Th.	Ar.........Pierre.........Ar.	5:25 PM Mo.
7:40 AM Fr.	Ar.....Rapid City....Lv.	9:00 PM Mo.
Ex. Sun.		**256** Ex. Sun.
10:45 AM Fr.	Ar...Belle Fourche..Lv.	4:30 PM Mo.

In this November 9, 1963, photo an A-B-B-A configuration of North Western F-units is rolling east over Great Northern trackage bound for St. Paul and beyond to Altoona, Wisconsin. (William S. Kuba)

CHICAGO - JANESVILLE - BELOIT - MADISON

Northbound—Read Down / Southbound—Read Up

591	Example	595 Ex. Sat.	Example	TABLE 15		578 Ex. Sun.	Example	594	Example
10:00 AM Mo.		11:00 PM Mo.		Lv..Chicago (Proviso)..Ar.		1:00 AM Tu.		12:45 AM Tu.	
1:00 PM Mo.		2:30 AM Tu.		Ar.....Harvard.....Ar.		10:30 PM Mo.		10:28 PM Mo.	
4:00 PM Mo.				Ar......Beloit......Ar.				8:35 PM Mo.	
6:00 PM Mo.				Ar.....Madison.....Lv.				5:45 PM Mo.	
....		4:00 AM Tu.		Ar.....Janesville.....Lv.		8:00 PM Mo.		....	

MILWAUKEE - MADISON

Westbound—Read Down / Eastbound—Read Up

669 Ex. Sun.	Example	TABLE 16		668 Ex. Sat.	Example
8:05 AM Mo.		Lv.....Milwaukee....Ar.		3:00 PM Mo.	
8:55 AM Mo.		Ar.....Waukesha.....Ar.		2:00 PM Mo.	
10:28 AM Mo.		Ar.....Jefferson Jct.....Ar.		10:25 AM Mo.	
2:45 PM Mo.		Ar......Madison.....Lv.		8:20 AM Mo.	

GREEN BAY - ALTOONA

Westbound—Read Down / Eastbound—Read Up

71 Dly. Ex. Sun.	Example	TABLE 17		72 Dly. Ex. Sun.	Example
3:30 AM Mo.		Lv..North Green Bay..Ar.		12:01 AM Tu.	
7:00 AM Mo.		Ar.......Eland......Ar.		6:00 PM Mo.	
10:00 AM Mo.		Ar......Wausau.....Ar.		5:00 PM Mo.	
1:00 PM Mo.		Ar.....Marshfield....Ar.		12:30 PM Mo.	
8:30 PM Mo.		Ar......Altoona.....Lv.		9:30 AM Mo.	

DES MOINES - MINNEAPOLIS

Northbound—Read Down / Southbound—Read Up

66-67-55-46-20	Example	TABLE 18		17-45-54-68-65	Example
66 Ex. Mo.				65 Ex. Sun.	
3:00 AM Tu.		Lv....Des Moines....Ar.		2:00 AM We.	
6:00 AM Tu.		Ar.....Ames.....Ar.		12:30 AM We.	
6:50 AM Tu.		Ar......Jewell......Lv.		11:15 PM Tu.	
67 Ex. Mo.				68 Ex. Sun.	
7:05 AM Tu.		Lv......Jewell......Ar.		11:00 PM Tu.	
8:30 AM Tu.		Ar...Eagle Grove..Lv.		9:30 PM Tu.	
55 Ex. Sun.				54 Ex. Sun.	
9:00 AM Tu.		Lv....Eagle Grove...Ar.		6:30 PM Tu.	
1:05 PM Tu.		Ar......Elmore.....Lv.		2:15 PM Tu.	
46 Ex. Sun.				45 Ex. Sun.	
1:30 PM We.		Lv......Elmore.....Ar.		10:45 AM Tu.	
5:30 PM We.		Ar.....Mankato.....Lv.		6:20 AM Tu.	
20 Daily				17 Daily	
11:00 PM We.		Lv.....Mankato.....Ar.		4:00 AM Tu.	
3:30 AM Th.		Ar. West Minneapolis Lv.		11:59 PM Mo.	

SIOUX CITY - HURON - OAKES

Westbound—Read Down / Eastbound—Read Up

23-1 Ex. Sun.	Example	TABLE 19		2 Ex. Sun.	Example
3:55 PM Tu.		Lv.....Sioux City....Ar.		3:35 AM Tu.	
5:00 PM Tu.		Ar.....Hawarden.....Ar.		2:00 AM Tu.	
10:40 PM Tu.		Ar......Huron.....Lv.		8:45 PM Mo.	
2:30 AM We.		Lv.......Huron.....Ar.		5:15 PM Mo.	
7:00 AM We.		Ar.....Aberdeen.....Ar.		2:25 PM Mo.	
9:30 AM We.		Ar........Oakes.....Lv.		12:15 PM Mo.	

CHICAGO - SIOUX CITY - SIOUX FALLS

Westbound—Read Down / Eastbound—Read Up

261-44	Example	TABLE 20		45-256	Example
6:30 PM Mo.		Lv..Chicago (Proviso).Ar.		11:45 AM Tu.	
2:30 PM Tu.		Ar....Missouri Valley..Ar.		10:45 PM Mo.	
44				45	
10:30 PM Tu.		Lv....Missouri Valley...Ar.		9:30 PM Mo.	
....		Ar....California Jct....		....	
....		Lv....California Jct....		....	
6:00 AM We.		Ar......Sioux City.....Lv.		7:30 PM Mo.	

CHICAGO - LINCOLN - SUPERIOR

Westbound—Read Down / Eastbound—Read Up

261-117-143-339	Example	TABLE 21		340-144-256-252	Example
				252 Daily	
6:30 PM Mo.		Lv. Chicago (Proviso)..Ar.		9:00 PM We.	
2:30 PM Tu.		Ar...Missouri Valley..Lv.		5:30 AM We.	
117-143 Dly. Ex. Sun.				144-256 Ex. Mon.	
10:30 PM Tu. Ex. Mon.		Lv...Missouri Valley..Ar.		8:30 PM Tu. Ex. Sun.	
11:30 PM Tu.		Ar......Fremont.....Lv.		6:00 PM Tu.	
12 Noon We.		Ar......Lincoln.....Lv.		1:00 PM Tu.	
339 Mon. Wed. Fri.				340 Tu. Thu. Sat.	
3:50 PM We.		Ar......Superior.....Lv.		11:45 AM Tu.	

CRANES AND DERRICKS

LOCATION	TYPE	CAPACITY	
Antigo, Wisconsin	Derrick	5	Ton
Appleton, Wis.	Derrick	10	Ton
Ashland, Wis.	Crane	1½	Ton
Ashland, Wis.	Derrick	5	Ton
Chadron, Nebr.	Derrick	2	Ton
Chadron, Nebr.	Air Hoist	2	Ton
Council Bluffs, Iowa	Derrick	5	Ton
Escanaba, Michigan	Derrick	1	Ton
Fond Du Lac, Wis.	Derrick	1	Ton
Green Bay, Wis.	Derrick	1½	Ton
Hurley, Wisconsin	Crane	1¼	Ton
Huron, S.D.	Derrick	6	Ton
Manitowoc, Wis.	Derrick	5	Ton
Manitowoc (Calumet Yd) Wis.	Derrick	1	Ton
Milwaukee, Wis. (Jackson St.)	Derrick	5	Ton
Milwaukee, Wis. (3rd Ward)	Derrick with Hoist	15	Ton
Omaha, Nebr.	Transfer Crane	30	Ton
Oshkosh, Wis.	Derrick	10	Ton
Proviso, Ill.	Gantry Crane	10	Ton
Sheboygan, Wis.	Gantry Crane	6	Ton
Sioux City, Iowa	Gantry Crane	10	Ton
Wausau, Wis.	Derrick	5 and 10	Ton

TRACK SCALES
At the Following C&NW Railway Stations

Adams, Wis.
Altoona, Wis.
Antigo, Wis.
Appleton, Wis.
Ashland, Wis.
Baraboo, Wis.
Belle Plaine, Ia.
Beloit, Wis.
Belvidere, Ill.
Boone, Ia.
Butler, Wis.
Casper, Wyo.
Cedar Rapids, Ia.
Chadron, Neb.
Chicago, Ill.
Clinton, Ia.
Clintonville, Wis.
Council Bluffs, Ia.
Crystal Lake, Ill.
Cudahy, Wis.
DeKalb, Ill.
Des Moines, Ia.
Eagle Grove, Ia.
East Minneapolis, Minn.
East Elgin, Ill.
Eau Claire, Wis.
Elroy, Wis.
Escanaba, Mich.
Fond du Lac (North Yard), Wis.
Fremont, Neb.
Green Bay (North Yard), Wis.
Hawarden, Ia.
Hudson, Wis.
Hurley, Wis.
Huron, S. D.
Iron Mountain, Mich.
Iron River, Mich.
Ishpeming, Mich.
Itasca, Wis.
Ives, Wis.
Kenosha, Wis.
La Crosse, Wis.
Laona, Wis.
Lincoln, Neb.
Long Pine, Neb.
Madison, Wis.
Manitowoc, Wis.
Mankato, Minn.
Marinette, Wis.
Marshalltown, Ia.
Marshfield, Wis.
Mason City, Ia.
Milwaukee, Wis.
Minneapolis, Minn. (Plymouth Yard)
Neenah, Wis.
Norfolk Neb.
Oconto, Wis.
Omaha, Neb.
Oshkosh, Wis.
Pierre, S. D.
Proviso, Ill.
Racine, Wis.
Rapid City, S. D.
Rhinelander, Wis.
Rice Lake, Wis.
Rockford, Ill.
Sacton, Ia.
St. James, Minn.
St. Paul, Minn.
Shawano, Wis.
Sheboygan, Wis.
Sioux City, Ia.
Sioux Falls, S. D.
South Beloit, Ill.
South Janesville, Wis.
South Pekin, Ill.
Spooner, Wis.
Sterling, Ill.
Tama, Ia.
Wakefield, Mich.
Waseca, Minn.
Washburn, Wis.
Watersmeet, Mich.
Watertown, S. D.
Waukegan, Ill.
Waukesha, Wis.
Wausau, Wis.
West Chicago, Ill.
Winona, Minn.
Worthington, Minn.

Alco RS3 No. 1554 teams up with No. 1515, switching Train 495 prior to departing Waseca for Tracy and Huron over the Waseca Subdivision of the Central Division. No. 1554 was the second such unit on the C&NW to carry that number—this No. 1554 was the former Litchfield & Madison No. 303 and was the last RS3 to be built. (William S. Kuba)

right: Train No. 62 is on the Madison Sub. of the Wisconsin Division near North Freedom. (Dr. F. W. De Sautelle, Author's Collection)

below: GP9s 1756 and 1730 on a tank-car train. (C&NW)

facing page, top to bottom: GP9 No. 1771 leads two ex-CGW GP30s north at Belle Plaine, Minn., en route from Sioux City to Minneapolis on September 22, 1970.

Rebuilt GP9 4502 (ex-M&StL No. 600) on the former M&StL main line at Albion, Iowa, on September 30, 1972.

F-units lead Extra 425 West at Kenosha, Wis., on August 17, 1974.

F3A No. 239—rolling into Albert Lea, Minn., over the Albert Lea Subdivision of the Central Division on June 30, 1972—is ex-Florida East Coast No. 508. (All, W. S. Kuba)

AlphaTrain symbols during the 1980s. (For Overland Route trains see Chapter 3.)

TABLE 1	
Train Symbols (for both directions)	**Terminals**
MTGCA /GCMTA	Marshalltown–Alton & Southern Yard
DWKCA / KCDWA	Superior/Duluth (DW&P)–Kansas City
EMMTA / MTEMA	East Minneapolis–Marshalltown
EMNPA / NPEMA	East Minneapolis–Council Bluffs
PRBEA /BEBIA	Proviso Yard–Belvidere
BRADA /ADBRA	Clearing Yard (BRC)–Adams
PREMT / EMPRA	Proviso Yard–East Minneapolis
PRDWA / DWPRA	Proviso Yard–Duluth/Superior (DW&P)
PREMA / EMPRA	Proviso Yard–ast Minneapolis
PRGBB / GBPRA	Proviso Yard–Green Bay
PRGBA / GBPTA	Proviso Yard–Green Bay
FDGBB / GBFDA	Fond du Lac–Green Bay
PRKNA / KNPRA	Kaukauna–Proviso Yard
ADRCA / RCADA	Adams–Rapid City
PRMWA / MWPTA	Proviso Yard–Madison
PRJAB / JAPRB	Proviso Yard–Janesville
PRJAA / JAPRA	Proviso Yard–Janesville
PRNZA / NZPRA	Proviso Yard–Mitchell Yard (Milwaukee)
PRBUA / BUPRB	Proviso Yard–Butler (Milwaukee)
BUJJA / JJBUA	Butler–Jefferson Junction
FTMCA / MCFTA	Fort Dodge–Mason City
GBESA / ESGBA	Green Bay–Escanaba
ESISA / ISESA	Escanaba–Ishpeming
GBFDB / FDGBA	Green Bay–Fond du Lac
FDEMA / EMFDA	Fond du Lac–East Minneapolis
FTDMA / DMFTA	Fort Dodge–Des Moines
HUOKA / OKHUA	Huron–Oakes

above: In 1968 the C&NW purchased seven U30C's from General Electric. No. 936 leads an eastbound train past East St. Paul yard office en route to Altoona (Eau Claire) and beyond on May 31, 1968.

right: A southbound extra is adding tonnage at Mitchell Yard for the remainder of its trip to Chicago over the New Line Subdivision. A "trademark" of C&NW motive power was the gong-style nose bell on many of the GP and SD low-nose units, as is visible here on SD40-2 No. 6853. (Both, William S. Kuba)

bottom: The C&NW line to Duluth-Superior once played an important role in Canadian National (DW&P) interchange traffic. Upon its arrival at Duluth on March 23, 1974, a C&NW transfer crew brought this CN train from the DW&P to Superior's Itasca Yard. In this view, the train was rolling over the C&NW as Extra 6850 South en route to Milwaukee. (Author)

left: A local freight on the ex-Rock Island "Spine Line" crosses the Chicago Central at Mills Tower, north of Iowa Falls on the Iowa Falls Subdivision of the Central Division on July 31, 1982.

middle: The C&NW's grain traffic covered a wide area west of the Mississippi River on virtually all routes. Here an empty grain train is approaching Eagle Grove, Iowa, on the Jewell Subdivision of the Central Division on June 20, 1983. The Jewell Sub. connected with a branch to Bancroft (the Burt Subdivision) and a line west to Marathon on the Laurens Sub. Both lines were part of the Central Division, with many grain elevators throughout the area.

below: The east-west line from Winona to Rapid City was also once an important source of C&NW grain traffic. Train ADHUA (Adams–Huron) is shown here at Waseca, Minnesota, on April 24, 1986. (All, William S. Kuba)

right: Paper traffic was important for the C&NW in central and northern Wisconsin. Local No. WWN33 (Wisconsin Rapids to Nekoosa and return) is rolling through Port Edwards, Wis., en route to Nekoosa on May 21, 1988.

middle: An eastbound local rolls through Jordon, Minn., on the ex-Omaha Road between the Twin Cities and Sioux City. During the mid- to late 1980s this local was designated WWNO4 from Montgomery north, with its west-bound counterpart designated WWNO5 from the Twin Cities back to Montgomery.

below: Symbol freight HUADA (the former Train 482) charges out of the Soo Line (ex-Milwaukee Road) tunnel at Tunnel City, Wis., on May 21, 1988. The C&NW's own trackage had been abandoned between Tunnel City and Winona, and thus the company operated over ex-Milwaukee Road trackage between those points. (All, William S. Kuba)

above: Three SD18s with a grain train are being held just outside of Valley Park, Minn., on the former Omaha Road on April 17, 1985.

middle: Train KMDWA began before 1974 as Trains 164 (Kansas City to Minneapolis) and 461 (to Duluth-Superior). The schedule was combined in 1981 to form KCDWA; it was later redesignated KMDWA and operated on a daily basis. KMDWA—shown here at Coon Creek Junction on April 18, 1989—handled traffic for Des Moines, Iowa Falls, Mason City, Mankato, Minneapolis, and Duluth for connection with the DW&P (CN). The train originated at Missouri Pacific's Armstrong Yard. (Both, William S. Kuba)

left: Union Pacific power was common on the C&NW over the years. In this case, Train 471, en route from Green Bay to Minneapolis in December 1978, is running as Extra UP 3112 West near Hazel Park Junction in east St. Paul. (Author)

top: C&NW No. 1036, in full yellow-and-green striping and bearing the "Route of the Streamliners" slogan, was an H10-44 switcher built at Beloit, Wisconsin, by Fairbanks-Morse in November 1944. (F-M, Kevin J. Holland Collection)

middle: Among the less-remarked members of the diesel switcher fleet were the Baldwin engines, such as No. 99, which belonged to the Omaha Road. The C&NW operated a variety of switch engines in the Northland at Duluth, Superior, Ashland, and the Twin Cities. Omaha engines shared the yellow-and-green scheme with the slogan "Route of the 400," plus CStPM&O sublettering on the lower section of the cab. (Northern Illinois University C&NW Archives Collection)

bottom: Alco S-2 No. 1027 is in its final, simplified color scheme as it performs classification work at Altoona Yard in Eau Claire, Wisconsin. (Bob Lorenz)

above: Just southeast of downtown St. Paul, the Milwaukee Road, Burlington, and the C&NW operated yard facilities. Here, three Geeps led by No. 4556 are pulling a transfer out of the C&NW's yard located next to the Mississippi River, while a BN coal train heads eastbound on the joint Milwaukee Road (now Soo/Canadian Pacific) main line in September 1984. (William S. Kuba)

middle: Going back a few years to the 1970s—September 1976 to be exact—many transfers were handled by switch engines. This East St. Paul Yard transfer was departing the Dayton's Bluff area, southeast of downtown St. Paul, behind a C&NW "cow and calf" EMD pair. (Author's Collection)

bottom: There was always a great variety of train action at St. Paul. As a C&NW transfer led by GP7 No. 1634 moves toward the North Western yard, Burlington Northern SD24s led by No. 6241 are handling a transfer for both the BN's yard and the Milwaukee Road's yard in August 1974. (William S. Kuba)

31

3

The Overland Route

The "Overland Route" was the name given to joint Chicago–San Francisco freight and passenger services operated by three railroads: the Chicago & North Western (between Chicago and Council Bluffs/Omaha), the Union Pacific (between Omaha and Ogden, Utah), and the Southern Pacific (between Ogden and the Pacific coast). After October 1955, the Milwaukee Road replaced C&NW as the Overland Route's eastern passenger-service segment.

The C&NW's Chicago–Omaha segment of the Overland Route played a major role in connection Union Pacific's freight services for several generations. In fact, this was the case right up until the C&NW-UP merger in 1995. The Omaha–Chicago trackage was a natural connection for the UP.

What did some of these freight services look like? An entire book could be written about the

C&NW-UP freight connections from their very beginning in the 1860s. This particular chapter will look at the variety of train operations during the last 50 years of the C&NW from 1945 through 1995.

The C&NW began a freight-train schedule improvement program as the year 1946 progressed. One of the first time freights to be speeded up between Chicago and Council Bluffs (Omaha) was No. 251, which was named the *Round-up*. The train's schedule was reduced by six hours between Chicago and Council Bluffs. Two other trains providing overnight freight services included the *Aksarben*, from Chicago to Ames and Boone, Iowa; and the *Calumet*, from Council Bluffs to Clinton, Illinois.

Throughout the 1950s and early 1960s, the C&NW operated a minimum of four scheduled time freights each way between Chicago and Council Bluffs—the Union Pacific transfer. The fastest westbound train was No. 249, scheduled from Chicago to Council Bluffs in ten hours, 30 minutes (10:00 a.m. to 8:30 p.m.). The fastest eastbound train was No. 258, scheduled for 13 hours (10:30 a.m. to 11:30 p.m.).

Freight train traffic continued to increase on the Overland Route out of Chicago. By the mid-1970s there were five trains each way daily for the Union Pacific connection alone. But that was only part of the picture on the main line. There were five trains daily, or at least six days a week, for the Chicago–Iowa services including three each way Chicago–Council Bluffs. There were three additional trains each way between Chicago and Nelson en route to and from St. Louis. The Chicago–Kansas City traffic included two trains each way daily between Chicago and Marshalltown.

Four FT units in A-B-B-A formation power a solid train of refrigerator cars near Council Bluffs, Iowa, in the mid-1940s. The train included C&NW and Pacific Fruit Express cars along with "reefers" from the Santa Fe and other western railroads. (C&NW Photo, Author's Collection)

33

The Overland Route! Commonly thought of the "Route of the Streamliners," the Chicago–Omaha and Union Pacific connections played a major role in the C&NW's freight operations. In 2003, the Omaha–Chicago segment is still a vital part of the Union Pacific System's transcontinental services. Slipping back to the 1930s, the C&NW arranged a publicity photo of a trainload of automobiles en route from Pontiac, Michigan, to Oakland, California. Automobiles were handled in box cars in those days, whereas now the traffic is handled in tri-level auto rack cars. Motive power was 2-8-2 No. 421, a class J-A of the Omaha Road. (C&NW Photo, Author's Collection)

High-priority freight trains were provided with the most modern steam power. In October 1942, this eastbound freight was running fast with a 4-8-4 Northern doing the honors. The train was crossing the Indian Creek Bridge east of Cedar Rapids, Iowa. (Joe Sleger, William S. Kuba Collection)

34

The number of trains in and out of Chicago totaled approximately 30 per day, or 15 each way. (Depending whether the trains operated five, six, or seven days per week.)

The train numbers, origins and destinations were as follows:

Transcontinental Services—Westbound

241   Proviso–North Platte
(Empty refrigerator cars for the West)
243   Wood Street–LA
(*Los Angeles Falcon* Minimum 4 Days/Week)
245   Wood St.–LA, Oakland, Seattle
(*The Falcon*)
247   Proviso–All West Coast Points
249   Proviso–All West Coast Points

The C&NW operated on the left side of their double-track main lines, as observed here with a 4-8-4 Northern handling an eastbound freight at Lisbon, Iowa, 201 miles west of Chicago in Automatic Train Control Territory. (Joe Sleger, William S. Kuba Collection)

Extra 2594 East is passing the depot at Mt. Vernon, Iowa, 203.3 miles west of Chicago. The crew has 65.2 miles to go to reach Clinton, Iowa, and Mississippi River crossing into the state of Illinois. It is November 15, 1942, and the eastbound extra is a reflection of heavy wartime traffic. (Joe Sleger, William S. Kuba Collection)

below: A westbound freight rolls through Ames, Iowa with a 4-8-4 Northern for power. The big engines had the responsibility of keeping the time freights on time for connections with the Union Pacific. The photo was taken from the interlocking tower, date unknown. (Don Christiansen, William S. Kuba Collection)

bottom: A westbound extra departs the Boone, Iowa, yard with a hefty train for Omaha in the 1940s. Note the street crossing tower, which of course is a scene that has completely disappeared from the railroad industry throughout North America. (William S. Kuba Collection)

Transcontinental Services—Eastbound

246	All West Coast points–Proviso (Perishable Manifest from SP, WP, UP connecting with Penn Central)
248	West Coast points–Wood Street (*Wood Street Falcon* TOFC/Perishable Special to B&O, C&O, EL, GTW, and N&W)
250	Denver–Wood Street (TOFC/Manifest/Perishable connecting B&O, C&O, EL, GTW, and N&W)
252	West Coast points–Proviso (Wisconsin destinations and Penn Central)
256	Denver–Proviso (Wisconsin destinations)

Chicago–St. Louis trains included:

381,397	Proviso–Madison, Illinois
383	Proviso–Alton & Southern Yard
380	Madison–Chicago
386	Alton & Southern Yard–Proviso

Chicago–Kansas City

141,143	Proviso–Kansas City
142,144	Kansas City–Proviso

Chicago–Iowa Services

251,253,255	Proviso–Council Bluffs
259	Proviso–Clinton
261	Proviso–Beverly, Iowa
254	Council Bluffs–Chicago 40th St.
256	Council Bluffs–Proviso
258	Council Bluffs–Wood Street
260	Clinton–Proviso
262	Marshalltown–Proviso

When adding extra freights and other unscheduled movements, the number of trains often exceeded 30 on the Nelson–Proviso segment of the eastern end of the Overland Route.

The New Letter Train Symbols

The year 1980 marked the beginning of a new system for train scheduling and designations. Planning began for the new alpha symbol system as described in Chapter 2. For the Overland Route, this meant a system that would match the new Union Pacific symbols, part of which had to do with the merger with the Missouri Pacific.

CHICAGO - COUNCIL BLUFFS - OMAHA

Westbound — TABLE 1

Note: All schedules are planned to provide fast through connections with all carriers from Eastern Points.

	249	Example	255	Example	251	Example	261	Example	253	Example
Lv. Chicago (Proviso)...	10:00 AM Mo.		11:00 PM Mo.		2:00 PM Mo.		6:30 PM Mo.		8:00 AM Mo.	
Ar. West Chicago......									8:30 AM Mo.	
Ar. De Kalb......									10:00 AM Mo.	
Ar. Nelson......					4:30 PM Mo.				11:00 AM Mo.	
Ar. Sterling......									1:00 PM Mo.	
Ar. Clinton......	12:45 PM Mo.		2:00 AM Tu.		6:00 PM Mo.		1:00 AM Tu.		5:00 PM Mo.	
Ar. Cedar Rapids......					9:00 PM Mo.		4:00 AM Tu.		2:00 AM Tu.	
Ar. Belle Plaine......							6:00 AM Tu.		5:00 AM Tu.	
Ar. Marshalltown......									7:30 AM Tu.	
Ar. Boone......	5:00 PM Mo.		7:15 AM Tu.		12:01 AM Tu.		9:15 AM Tu.		9:30 AM Tu.	
Ar. Missouri Valley......							2:30 PM Tu.			
Ar. Council Bluffs......	8:30 PM Mo.		10:45 AM Tu.		5:30 AM Tu.		4:30 PM Tu.			
Ar. Union Pacific Transfer	10:30 PM Mo.		1:30 PM Tu.		7:30 AM Tu.		9:00 PM Tu.			
Ar. Omaha......							1:30 AM We.			

Note: Schedules are coordinated with Council Bluffs-Omaha Lines to effect fast through connections to Pacific Coast and intermediate points.

OMAHA - COUNCIL BLUFFS - CHICAGO

Eastbound — TABLE 2

Note: These schedules are planned to provide fast through connections with all Council Bluffs-Omaha lines from Pacific Coast and Intermediate Points.

	258	Example	252	Example	256	Example	254	Example	250 Daily Ex. Sat. and Sun.	Example
Lv. South Omaha......					7:00 PM Mo.					
Lv. North Omaha......			12:30 AM Mo.							
Lv. Union Pacific Transfer	9:50 AM Mo.				6:30 PM Mo.					
Lv. Council Bluffs......	10:30 AM Mo.		4:30 AM Mo.		9:15 PM Mo.		12:30 PM Mo.			
Ar. Missouri Valley......			5:30 AM Mo.		10:00 PM Mo.		1:30 PM Mo.			
Ar. Boone......	1:30 PM Mo.		9:30 AM Mo.		1:30 AM Tu.		6:00 PM Mo.			
Ar. Marshalltown......			12:01 PM Mo.		3:30 AM Tu.				Lv.	
Ar. Belle Plaine......					4:30 AM Tu.				5:00 PM Tu.	
Ar. Cedar Rapids......	5:00 PM Mo.		2:00 PM Mo.		5:00 AM Tu.		1:00 AM Tu.		6:00 PM Tu.	
Ar. Clinton......	7:30 PM Mo.		4:30 PM Mo.		7:30 AM Tu.		4:00 AM Tu.		9:00 PM Tu.	
Ar. Sterling......							5:45 AM Tu.			
Ar. Nelson......			6:30 PM Mo.				6:30 AM Tu.			
Ar. De Kalb......							8:00 AM Tu.			
Ar. West Chicago......							10:00 AM Tu.			
Ar. Chicago (Proviso)...	11:30 PM Mo.		9:00 PM Mo.		11:45 AM Tu.		11:30 AM Tu.		1:30 AM We.	

Note: Schedules are coordinated with Eastern Carriers to effect fast through connections to Eastern Points.

It is August 31, 1947, and still early in the dieselization process. A new C&NW F3A, No. 4051, leads two FT's and 87 cars on an eastbound run as it crosses the Burlington Route's Chicago–Minneapolis main line at Rochelle, Illinois. (Jim Scribbins)

above: F-units were replaced by GP7s and GP9s by the 1960s. By the time of this September 1970 view, the older Geeps have been replaced on time freights by newer GP30s, GP35s, and even SD40s. However, the older Geeps still had many jobs to do on the Overland Route. In this case, No. 1740 and its running mate are handling a 14-car local freight at Missouri Valley, Iowa, 463.7 miles west of Chicago in ATC territory.

middle: This particular time freight was crossing the multiple tracks of the Chicago Great Western and the Minneapolis & St. Louis routes on the west end of Marshalltown, Iowa, on October 27, 1962.

bottom: By the late 1970s—in this case, October 20, 1978—the through Chicago–UP freights were handled by SD40-2s like No. 6904 heading up this eastbound freight from Fremont, Nebraska, to Chicago. The train is at West Side, Iowa, 405.6 miles west of Chicago on the Overland Route. (All, William S. Kuba)

38

There were a few train number changes during the late 1970s and 1980, in part because of an increased frequency of train operations. The change from numbers to the new alpha system is summarized below.

Transcontinental Services—
Train No.	Alpha Symbol
239	WSSOT

Wood Street–Oakland, *The Falcon*, intermodal
| 243 | WSLAT |

Wood Street–LA intermodal
| 247 | PRNPT |

Proviso–North Platte, auto and intermodal
| 251 | PRNPB |

Proviso–North Platte
| 273 | ELNPA |

Blue Island, Ill.,–North Platte
| 275 | PINPA |

Blue Island–North Platte

(All westbound trains provided service for the Union Pacific connections.)

| 242 | LAWST |

LA–Wood Street, Intermodal
| 248 | NPWST |

North Platte–Wood Street *Wood Street Falcon*
| 250 | NPPTA |

North Platte–Proviso, manifest and perishable connection to the C&O, B&O, and N&W
| 252 | NPPRA |

North Platte–Proviso, run-through with UP and GTW Train 370
| 256 | NPPRB |

Second North Platte–Proviso with additional Iowa–Chicago service
| 274 | NPBIA |

North Platte–Blue Island, transcontinental perishable and manifest service via SP, WP, UP, and an eastern connection with Conrail
| 276 | NPBIB |

Second North Platte–Blue Island with same basic transcontinental service Conrail connection

Chicago–Iowa Services
Train No.	Alpha Symbol
255	PRCBA

Proviso–Council Bluffs
| 259 | PRCEA |

Proviso–Beverly

| 254 | BVPRA |

Beverly–Proviso
| 258 | CBPRA |

Council Bluffs–Proviso
| 272 | CBBIA |

Council Bluffs–Blue Island

Chicago–St. Louis Services
Train No.	Alpha Symbol
381	PRMAA

Proviso–Madison, Ill.
| 383 | PRGCA |

Proviso–Alton & Southern Yard

| 380 | MAPRA |

Madison–Proviso
| 386 | GCPRA |

Alton & Southern Yard–Proviso

Chicago–Wyoming Services
Train No.	Alpha Symbol
355	PRBFA

Proviso–Belle Fourche, S.D.
| 358 | BFPRA |

Belle Fourche–Proviso

In addition to the UP connection trains, the C&NW also handled a substantial amount of grain traffic over the Overland Route. GP50 No. 5070 leads an eastbound grain train as it approaches the single-track Cedar River Bridge after having met a series of westbound UP connection freights prior to resuming its eastward run on June 4, 1983. (William S. Kuba)

Chicago–Kansas City Services
Train No.	Alpha Symbol
141	PRKAA

Proviso–Kansas City
| 143 | PRKCA |

Proviso– Kansas City

| 142 | KAPRA |

Kansas City–Proviso
| 144 | KCPRA |

Kansas City–Proviso

These basic train services continued throughout the 1980s and early 1990s, right up to the Union Pacific merger. The Overland Route services expanded over time as intermodal and coal traffic continued to increase. Twenty years and more beyond the freight train symbol designation changes, the Overland Route of the former C&NW and, later, the Union Pacific is as busy as ever. The Railroad Park established by the town of Rochelle, Illinois, at the crossing of today's UP and BNSF main lines (photo above) is a great place to watch the "show" in comfort and safety.

At almost the exact same spot as the F-units shown on pages 36-37, a Chicago-bound time freight crosses the Burlington Northern diamonds at Rochelle, Illinois—74.8 miles west of Chicago in double-track territory—on August 12, 1988. (William S. Kuba)

A single SD50, No. 5094, handles an auto-rack train with a GTW box car of auto parts on the head end. This westbound train is of a high priority as it travels through Fairfax, Iowa, on July 9, 1981. (William S. Kuba)

top: Moving into the 1990s, motive power on the Overland Route continued to diversify. In addition to through UP units, various trains included Conrail power as well. Symbol train PRNPA (Proviso–North Platte) has eight units for its westbound run from Chicago to Fremont. The third unit is from Conrail. Train PRNPA was photographed at Luzerne, 248.9 miles west of Chicago, on October 19, 1991.

middle: Throughout the 1980s and into the early 1990s, C&NW SD40-2s, GP50s, and similar power handled the time freights between Chicago and the UP connection at Fremont, Nebraska. This westbound is nearing Marshalltown, Iowa, on September 16, 1989.

below: An eastbound loaded grain train at Bertram, Iowa, on August 5, 1989, was being led by No. 6000, an experimental SD45 with a "CAT" engine. (All, William S. Kuba)

4

Intermodal

The Chicago & North Western was a pioneering and prominent intermodal carrier in the Midwest. The company began offering such services on August 13, 1953, and would become famous over the following decades as the route of intermodal trains like the *Viking 400*, the *Falcons*, and the *Pacers*.

The C&NW traced its intermodal "roots" to that date in 1953, when two loaded highway trailers were loaded "piggyback" on a converted flat car in the late afternoon. The car was switched into a regularly scheduled freight train with delivery the next morning in Chicago. The trailers belonged to the C&NW's pick-up and delivery service which coordinated the local handling in both Chicago and Green Bay with the rail service between those points.

The company emphasized that the service was an intensive test to determine the potential

success of the innovation. The C&NW had converted four flat cars, each of which could handle two trailers. Ramps had been constructed at Green Bay and Proviso Yard (west of Chicago). The trailers were loaded with LCL (Less than Carload) shipments.

This humble beginning in 1953 was the foundation for new services. The C&NW launched piggyback operations between Chicago and the Twin Cities, and Chicago and Omaha, on November 10, 1953. Piggyback services were expanded to include Milwaukee one month later. The initial success of the new services prompted the C&NW to research the possibilities of truckload service.

A new piggyback service directly competitive with motor common carriers was announced with a rate proposal placed before the Western Trunk Line Committee in December 1953. The applica-

tion and plan included a new door-to-door service with the truck trailers handled on the flat cars. The initial service was offered between Chicago and Green Bay in early 1954.

The year 1954 was a banner time for the expansion of the C&NW piggyback services. The company began offering overnight LCL service between the Twin Cities and Duluth-Superior on April 28th. A map of the piggyback operations included routes between Chicago, Milwaukee, and Green Bay; Chicago and the Twin Cities; Chicago and Omaha; and a Twin Cities–Twin Ports (Duluth-Superior) operation.

By the end of 1954, the C&NW had converted 62 flat cars (each 53 feet, 6 inches long) and leased 125 trailers in the 24- and 32-foot-long categories. Furthermore, the railroad was offering trailerload services to Waukegan and the Fox River Valley, which included areas beyond Green

In the early days of piggyback service, the trailers were loaded and unloaded "circus ramp" style. The tractor drivers had the task of loading the trailers by backing them over several flat cars to the next loading spot. (C&NW Historical Society Archives)

Aerial views of the
Proviso Piggyback
Plaza, Chicago.
(C&NW Historical
Society Archives)

44

above: Night scene at the Proviso Piggyback Plaza.

left: Trailers were loaded throughout the day and night. Night loading is taking place at Proviso with a tractor placing a Gordon's trailer on a flat car. (Both, C&NW Historical Society Archives)

Bay such as Appleton, Depere, Neenah-Menasha, and Oshkosh. By February 1, 1955, the company expanded LCL service to Fond du Lac and Marshfield, Wisconsin. The roots had taken hold, and the service was growing.

An example of the new growth and development was reported by *Railway Age* in March 1955. Thirty-seven loaded truck trailers moved between Chicago and the Twin Cities on February 15 when the C&NW launched trailerload rates

between those points. The new service was on a daily overnight door-to-door service basis at truck-competitive rates.

On May 31, 1955, the C&NW launched an overnight LCL service between Chicago and St. Louis through a connection with the Litchfield & Madison Railroad. Other interline services were established with second-morning deliveries between the Twin Cities and Louisville, Kentucky, through a connection with the Monon Railroad;

below: This C&NW
photo illustrates the
design of the loading
ramps for trailer traf-
fic. The company had
quite a number of
such facilities through-
out the system. Many,
such as at Superior,
Wisconsin, were sim-
ply one track with one
ramp. All of the mini-
terminals, if one could
call them that, were
eventually discontin-
ued and dismantled.
(C&NW Historical
Society Archives)

and also second morning deliveries between the Twin Cities, Milwaukee, and Cincinnati through a connection with the Pennsylvania Railroad.

In October 1955, the C&NW announced plans for piggyback interchange services with ten eastern railroads. Service was provided between 41 C&NW stations and more than 800 stations on the Pennsylvania, Lackawanna, Lehigh Valley, Nickel Plate, Reading, Wabash, Western Maryland, Pittsburgh & West Virginia and Monon railroads. One example of the service was a third-morning delivery in each direction between the Twin Cities and New York City, via connection with the PRR.

The C&NW's roster of intermodal equipment by the end of 1955 included 175 converted flat cars, 225 leased trailers, and 12 mechanical refrigerator trailers. Traffic averaged about 75 trailers per day.

Another aspect of piggyback traffic development by the C&NW included various types of research. One example was the handling of tanker trucks. The company conducted a series of impact tests with two water-filled tank trailers mounted on Trailer Train flat cars with standard ACF (American Car & Foundry) trailer hitches. The tests were conducted during the spring of 1960, and the AAR Bureau of Explosives gave tentative approval in July 1960 for handling such traffic.

Although the C&NW had decided to discontinue its LCL business in 1958, there was continued growth with their piggyback business into the 1960s. In 1963, the railroad built a new terminal, named the Proviso Piggyback Plaza, on the former land area of the LCL freight house. Built at a cost of $1.1 million, the new facility was officially opened for business on October 14, 1963. The

above: Several "cuts" of piggyback cars can be seen in this 1966 yard scene, while two GP35s and a GP30 idle in the foreground. (C&NW Historical Society Archives)

right: Many C&NW trailers carried the full railroad name, such as CNWZ 708157 riding on Trailer Train flat TTX 154956. (Author)

far right: Forty-foot trailers like ACWZ 200253, at Kansas City in April 1980, were common on the C&NW during the 1970s and 1980s. (Dennis Roos)

bottom: In April 1980, CNWZ 600011 wore the C&NW "Employee Owned" logo and the decorative flying Falcon. (Dennis Roos)

48

20-acre space provided parking areas for 330 highway trailers. The terminal included car-floor-level end loading docks serving 12 tracks. The new terminal replaced two Chicago-area facilities, one at the 40th Street Yard and the other at Proviso. Each of the former terminals contained but three tracks with an end-loading ramp.

The new Proviso Piggyback Plaza terminal could handle up to 700 highway trailers per day. Each of the tracks could accommodate eight 85-foot flat cars. The 12-track terminal could handle 96 flat cars at a time, with a maximum of 192 trailers on those flat cars. At the time of the terminal's construction, the C&NW's piggyback growth was averaging about 20 percent per year. Things would continue to be exciting.

The Falcons

Throughout the history of C&NW freight services, the company had been rather distinctive for naming freight trains. Consequently, when the new all-piggyback, through-train operations of the C&NW and UP went into service in 1973, it was not too much of a surprise when a name—*Falcon*—was selected for the new trains. When the new service was launched it immediately attracted enough new traffic to increase the company's annual loadings by 50 percent.

During the first year of *Falcon* operation, the C&NW operated one basic train in each direction on a daily basis between Chicago and the UP connection at Fremont, Nebraska. Except for the recession in 1975, the C&NW-UP operation gained new business every year. To handle the new and expanding piggyback traffic, at first the C&NW simply operated extra trains with high-speed performance. By 1977, however, the traffic levels required some new thinking for scheduling and precision performance. This came about by designating the trains as first-class schedules in the operating timetables. This meant that the *Falcons* had rights over all other trains, and other train crews were required to check the train registers at intermediate terminals to determine whether all scheduled first-class trains had arrived and/or departed.

When the new *Falcon* schedules were first placed in effect, the C&NW scheduled two westbounds and one eastbound daily, Nos. 243, 245, and 242, respectively. As business continued to increase, the *Falcons* required three westbound and three eastbound schedules on a daily basis by 1980. The fast westbound *Falcons* were numbered 239, 243, and 245; while the eastbounds were Nos. 242, 244, and 248. Even these three west-

bound and three eastbound schedules were sometimes not enough. When this happened, the trains were run in multiple sections, ie., First 239, Second 239, and so on. It was an interesting reminder of the days of passenger train operations when North Western trains such as the *Challenger* operated in multiple sections.

The *Falcons* were authorized to operate at a maximum 70 miles per hour over most sections of the Chicago, Illinois, and Iowa Divisions between Chicago and Fremont. Except for the separate line into the Wood Street intermodal terminal, and the route between Missouri Valley and Fremont, the *Falcons* traveled over the famous Overland Route of the once-famous *City* Streamliners and Domeliners. The Chicago–Omaha section of the C&NW had one of the highest speed limits for freight trains to be found anywhere in North America.

There were some interesting operating rules and procedures connected with the 70-mph operations. Since an Automatic Train Control (ATC) system was in use on the Overland Route, the lead unit for each train had to be equipped with an ATC device set for increased speeds and a brake pipe feed valve set for 90 pounds. The piggyback trains could consist of no more than 60 cars, and all cars had to be equipped with roller-bearing

With three GP50s for power, this westbound intermodal train has arrived at Fremont, Nebraska, and is ready to change crews and roll westward over the Union Pacific. Stretching around the curve, the entire train consists of trailers on September 18, 1981. (William S. Kuba)

trucks, exclusive of the caboose. The *Falcons* could handle only trailers, containers, or multi-level automobile-carrying cars. The trains were scheduled as fast as nine hours, 30 minutes for the 497-mile run between Chicago and Fremont. Some of the trains were slightly slower, but overall the *Falcons* averaged close to 50 mph for the entire distance.

above: With a variety of truck trailers for loads, an eastbound intermodal train crosses the Cedar River at Cedar Rapids, Iowa, on October 1, 1983.

right: On June 19, 1982, SD40-2 No. 6901 and a Union Pacific unit power an eastbound intermodal train around the curve at the base of Mt. Vernon Hill near Bertram, Iowa. A major portion of the train consists of Western Pacific and Union Pacific trailers bound for Chicago and points east.

bottom: C&NW intermodal trains on the Overland Route were often led by a mixture of motive power from more than one railroad. In this case, SD40-2 No. 6886 is joined by a Conrail unit for part of the transcontinental run. The eastbound train is crossing the Milwaukee Road's Ottumwa branch at Cedar Rapids, Iowa, on April 26, 1980. (All, William S. Kuba)

Falcon operations were changed again in 1982 when the through trains reverted to running as extra trains, but with a priority status and with letter symbols replacing the previous numbers. As explained in Chapter 2, the new alpha train symbol system was designed to be integrated with the through-train operations of the Union Pacific as follows:

Westbound
239   WSOAT
243   WSLAT
245   WSLAV

Eastbound
242   LAWST
244   OAWSV
248   NPWST

The letter symbols can be interpreted as follows: WS=Wood Street, OA=Oakland, LA=Los Angeles, and NP=North Platte, while T and V stand for "trailers" and "vans," respectively.

The six trains listed above were not the only piggyback trains on the Illinois and Iowa Divisions. The fleet also included:

SECRT   Seattle–Conrail Trailers
CROAT   Conrail–Oakland Trailers
LACRT   Los Angeles–Conrail Trailers
WSNPT   Wood Street–N. Platte Trailers
PRNPT   Proviso–North Platte Trailers

In addition to these trains, the trains formerly numbered 239 and 243 often ran with advance sections while the former 244 and 248 frequently ran with second sections with the appropriate letter symbols.

In addition to the fast trains, which were operating in the neighborhood of 95% on-time performance, the heart of the *Falcon* services could be found at the Wood Street Terminal. This terminal was responsible for loading the trailers and containers, preparing the trains, and pumping them out on time so that the main lines of the Chicago, Illinois, and Iown Divisions could handle the traffic to and from the UP at Fremont.

Wood Street was a former potato traffic terminal and during the 1980s consisted of 14 short tracks for loading piggyback cars. It turned out that this track layout was very productive at that time for loading and unloading intermodal cars. Each track could be used as a destination classification track for Los Angeles, San Francisco Bay Area, Portland, Seattle, Denver, and other points. With the short tracks, the C&NW could load trailers for the designated points on the particular tracks. Consequently, when it was time to make up the train, the switch crews could simply assem-

ble the different tracks' cars in the correct order. The terminal was an efficient intermodal classification yard simply because it was made up of multiple short tracks instead of a few long ones.

More than track arrangement alone made the Wood Street Terminal so productive. The intermodal flat cars were loaded and unloaded by FWD "Piggy-packers." These machines, which have been around since the early 1980s, can be compared to a giant fork-lift truck. They can load a container or a trailer aboard a flat car in a fraction of the time it once took to drive the trailers aboard using tractors and "circus-style" end-loading ramps. Unloading is even faster.

The *Falcons* were given special care prior to departure. Air hose connections were taped together for additional safety and the train care-

top: An eastbound intermodal train powered by three GP50s (designed for high speed freight service) crossing the Mississippi River at East Clinton, Illinois. On-time operation was and is essential for such trains.

above: This westbound Overland Route double stack train for the Union Pacific rolls over what was once termed the "Lane Cut-off" in South Omaha on August 15, 1986. (Both, William S. Kuba)

above: Sometimes motive power combinations on the C&NW could be a bit unexpected. In this case, GP50 No. 5060 leads a Conrail SD45. The eastbound train is heading up the hill at Bertram, Iowa, on May 20, 1989.

right: Two GP50s lead a westbound intermodal train with a Milwaukee Road trailer on the head end as the train approaches Belle Plaine, Iowa, on July 22, 1988.

bottom: This eastbound train is actually a mixed autorack and TOFC consist. It has just crossed the famed Kate Shelly Bridge, west of Boone, Iowa, on August 4, 1990. (All, William S. Kuba)

A westbound double-stack train passed Westside, Iowa, on June 17, 1992. Westside is the watershed between the Missouri and Des Moines Rivers. C&NW SD40-2 No. 6888 led two Union Pacific units on this priority train. (William S. Kuba)

fully checked for any malfunctions. The purpose of the extra work was to eliminate any potential problems—such as parted air hoses—to ensure on-time delivery to the Union Pacific.

During the late 1970s and early 1980s, there were other intermodal developments on the Overland Route—the route of the *Falcons*. For example, in May 1976 the C&NW and UP were awarded a U.S. Mail contract. Yes, the mail was back on track but this time in the form of trailer-on-flat-car (TOFC) instead of the box-express cars of decades past. The new mail business consisted of about 32,000 trailers per year, or about 87 trailers of mail per day at that time. The train was designated as the *Overland Mail* between Chicago and Seattle.

The new concept launched with the *Falcons* continued to bring in business for the C&NW. From the original one train per day each way in 1973, the company was operating an average of

22 *Falcons* westbound per week, with 12 eastbound, in 1977. The maximum *Falcon* operating consist at the time was 50 cars. A comfortable consist was considered to be in the 35- to 40-car range, with four locomotives.

From the 1980s, traffic continued to climb and included run-through motive power with the Union Pacific. The Overland Route intermodal trains eventually handled double-stack cars as well as traffic to and from ocean vessels on the west coast for Asia. The C&NW-UP participated in transcontinental "land-bridge" traffic between Asia and Europe by handling through trains to and from the eastern carriers. Eventually, the trains lost their cabooses—both run-through Union Pacific cars as well as the green-and-yellow C&NW cars. The UP-C&NW merger in 1995 ended the era of C&NW operations on the Overland Route, but in 2003 the Overland Route is still the home of fast intermodal trains.

It is November 11, 1994, and this westbound double- stack train has just changed crews at Clinton, Iowa. A C&NW SD50 (7020) and an SD60 (8034) are doing the job of keeping this train on time as it races for the UP connection at Fremont. For C&NW, 1994 was the last full year of independence; 1995 fulfilled Union Pacific's merger plans. (William S. Kuba)

Twin Cities–Los Angeles Piggyback Service

The excitement surrounding its new *Falcon* services prompted the C&NW to establish an all-piggyback service between the Twin Cities and Los Angeles in 1973. The trains connected with a section of the *Falcons* at Fremont, Nebraska. The new trains were named the *Viking South* and the *Viking North* and numbered 845 and 846, respectively. Despite a variety of efforts, the train did not secure the desired levels of traffic and was discontinued.

The Viking 400

The C&NW was quite happy with the success of the *Falcons*. Thus, the company began looking at other potential markets, and in mid-1977, the railroad launched the *Viking 400*, a name that brought back memories of the C&NW's passenger services.

The new train began operating overnight between Chicago and the Twin Cities six days a week. The train had a late cut-off time with a 7:30

right: This eastbound intermodal train has just changed crews with the Union Pacific at Fremont, Nebraska. The train was on the Blair line to Missouri Valley on June 18, 1992.

below: A westbound K-Lines double-stack train starts into the Bertram curve at Bertram, Iowa, with SD60 No. 8050 leading two Union Pacific units on this fast westbound run on June 20, 1992. (Both, William S. Kuba)

a.m. pick up time at both Proviso Yard in Chicago and Westminster Yard in St. Paul. The *Viking 400* trains had "rights" over all other trains over their entire route, and performed no intermediate work.

In anticipation of the new *Viking 400* service, the C&NW rebuilt Westminster Yard with three, 13-car-capacity tracks. The lease of a Piggypacker, the fifth to go into service for the company, permitted the yard to handle container traffic which could not have been handled by the former "circus" (end-loading) ramp.

The *Viking 400* did relatively well throughout the late 1970s, but was discontinued in 1980 as traffic dropped off substantially with the recession.

The Pacer

The newest train name on the C&NW was the *Pacer*, a new intermodal run placed in operation between Chicago and the Twin Cities in late 1981. The new *Pacer* operated once a day in each direction, Monday through Friday, with a cut-off time for trailers at 6 p.m., and a trailer availability for consignee pickup by noon the following day. The train was phased out by 1983.

C&NW Intermodal Wrap-Up

The company rebuilt a fleet of 53-foot flat cars to handle the new, longer trailers and containers hitting the road during the final years of the C&NW's existence as an independent railroad.

Trailer color schemes ranged from the early yellow-and-green to white or stainless steel with the C&NW insignia. Trailers and motive power both carried *Falcon* identification. At least two SD40-2 locomotives, Nos. 6922 and the 6910, were lettered for *Falcon* service complete with the flying falcon logo. An entire fleet of truck trailers was lettered for *Falcon* service.

As the C&NW promoted and developed its piggyback services, the company at one time had more than 90 ramps. By the end of 1977, however, the number had decreased to 43. The short-haul piggyback movements really did not catch on.

In terms of train traffic, the company operated more intermodal trains on the Overland Route during its last decade than it did passenger trains during the 1940s. And the same is true in 2003, but with Union Pacific power doing the honors on the head end!

C&NW and UP power led a westbound Maersk double-stack train around the curve at Bertram on Sept. 3, 1994.

This eastbound Maersk double-stack train is approaching Clinton, Iowa, en route from Fremont to Chicago over the C&NW on November 11, 1994. (Both, William S. Kuba)

5

Iron Ore

Some of the heaviest and most dramatic railroading to be found on the C&NW was on the rail lines leading to the Gogebic, Menominee, and Marquette iron ranges. The C&NW also handled taconite pellets to Escanaba, Michigan, and a variety of all-rail ore movements from the Mesabi Range. The three Michigan ranges provided the C&NW close to ten million tons of traffic every year. Although there have been many years when the ore business was very low, as during the Great Depression, the final decade of the C&NW's independence could be considered some of the best years ever.

The C&NW was merged into the Union Pacific Railroad in 1995, and great changes soon took place on the former North Western ore lines. None of the C&NW ore cars in Michigan were repainted with a Union Pacific insignia with C&NW reporting marks. The remainder of the

C&NW's ore lines in Michigan did not last long as part of the UP. In 1998 the lines north of Green Bay were sold to the Wisconsin Central, and were operated by WC subsidiary Sault Ste. Marie Bridge Company. Part of the C&NW ore car fleet was rebuilt with SSAM reporting marks. Canadian National purchased the Wisconsin Central in October 2001.

The C&NW Ore Lines

The C&NW was a creative and, in many ways, an unusual ore hauler. For example, during the 1940s and 1950s, 4-6-0 "Ten-Wheelers" were used at Ashland, Wisconsin, for switching the ore docks—very small engines indeed for such heavy work. Larger steam power, such as 2-8-0s and 2-8-2s, was used at Escanaba, Michigan. During the early days of dieselization, the C&NW sent 1000-horsepower Alco switchers to Ashland.

Meanwhile, at Escanaba, there was a mixture of C&NW and Milwaukee Road Fairbanks-Morse 1600-hp road switchers in use for the road trains, mine runs, and ore dock operations.

Other aspects of the C&NW ore traffic centered around the last wooden ore docks on the Great Lakes, the only iron ore port on Lake Michigan, the newest and most modern ore dock (a low-level dock), the ore car fleet, and the ore pooling agreements with the Soo Line and the Milwaukee Road. Although annual tonnages were less than those of the Duluth, Missabe & Iron Range Railway or the Great Northern (later part of Burlington Northern), the C&NW's ore operations had more variety and served a wider territory than either of these companies.

The Chicago & North Western was the first railroad in the Lake Superior region built specifically to handle iron ore from the mines to a lake

At one time there were four timber ore docks in operation in Escanaba, Michigan. C&NW dock No. 5's foundation can still be observed to the right of newer dock No. 6 in this 1964 view. The Milwaukee Road had also built two such docks to the north of the C&NW facilities. When the Milwaukee Road and the C&NW joined in an ore-traffic pool agreement in the 1930s, the Milwaukee Road docks were dismantled. (C&NW Photo, Author's Collection)

port for transfer to Great Lakes ore carriers. On April 22, 1862, the Peninsula Rail Road Company was organized to build a 62-mile line from Escanaba on Lake Michigan to the New Jackson Mine at Negaunee. The line was completed by the end of 1863, with the first movment of iron ore in the spring of 1864.

The Peninsula Rail Road was a construction subsidiary of the C&NW and the operation of the line was conducted by the parent company. The Peninsula line, by the way, was not physically connected with the parent company until 1872 when the main line from Green Bay reached Escanaba. During the time between 1864 and 1872, the lines were linked by a steamship operation between Green Bay and Escanaba.

In 1864, the first rail shipping season of iron ore in the Lake Superior region, the C&NW handled 31,072 tons of ore to the first Escanaba dock, known as the Merchants Dock. The dock was constructed in 1863 to handle iron ore and to receive supplies and materials for building the railroad. Within a few years, the railroad required a new dock and from that time until the early 1900s dock construction was one of the major industries in Escanaba. To keep pace with the growing size of the ore carriers, each new ore dock was generally higher, longer, and equipped with greater storage capacity and more pockets.

In 1884, when records were first maintained, 1,355,000 tons of iron ore moved through Escanaba and in the subsequent years only once, in 1932, did ore shipments through that port fall below one million tons. Since 1963, shipments have averaged more than six million tons annually.

Since 1864, over 400 million tons of iron ore have originated on the Menominee, Marquette, and Gogebic iron ranges and have been shipped through the port of Escanaba, in addition to Mesabi Range taconite pellets. This port on northern Lake Michigan is in a particularly strategic location because of its relative proximity to the steel mills on the lower Great Lakes.

With the exception of the present low-level dock, all of the Escanaba docks were similar in operation and design to other Lake Superior ore docks. Loaded cars of ore were moved over the top of the dock with the contents dumped into storage "pockets." When a boat arrived at the dock for loading, chutes connected to the pockets were lowered into the vessel's hold. With the opening of the pocket doors, the ore would flow though the chutes and into the vessel. Since 1863, when the Merchants dock was constructed, the following ore docks have been erected at Escanaba:

Dock No. 1

Built in 1871-72; 1,008 feet long by 37 feet high; 168 pockets; 16,800 tons storage capacity. Rebuilt in 1889; 1,104 feet long by 48-1/2 feet high; 184 pockets; 24,104 tons storage capacity. Dismantled in 1911-12.

Dock No. 2

Built in 1880-81; 1,152 feet long by 39-1/2 high; 192 pockets; 20,928 tons ore storage capacity. Dismantled in 1897.

Dock No. 3

Built in 1879-80; 1,200 feet long by 39-1/2 feet high; 200 pockets; 20,000 tons storage capacity. Rebuilt in 1895; 1,356 feet long by 52 feet, 8 inches high; 226 pockets; 30,284 tons storage capacity. This dock was destroyed by fire on October 24, 1924.

Dock No. 4

Built in 1887-88; 1,500 feet long by 48 feet high; 250 pockets; 32,750 tons ore storage capacity. Destroyed by fire on November 29, 1897. Reconstruction 1897-1898; 1,500 feet long by 59 feet high; 250 pockets; 32,750 tons capacity. Destroyed by the same fire that consumed No. 3 dock in October 1924.

Dock No. 5

Built in 1890-1891 for the Escanaba, Iron Mountain & Western Railway, a C&NW subsidiary; 1,392 feet long by 53 feet high; 232 pockets; 43,152 tons storage capacity. C&NW took over the operation of the dock shortly after its completion. Rebuilt in 1909-10; 2,220 feet long by 71 feet high; 370 pockets; 120,250 tons storage capacity. Retired shortly after World War II and dismantled in 1960.

Dock No. 6

Built in 1903; 1,920 feet long by 70 feet high; 320 pockets; 80,000 tons iron ore storage capacity. Reconstruction undertaken in 1924 with the same dimensions and capacity. Replaced by a new low-level dock in 1969.

Present Dock

Low-level 1,900-foot steel-and-concrete dock built on the foundation of the previous timber dock No. 6. Equipped with a traveling shiploader with a pivoting boom for loading vessels of all sizes, including the huge ore carriers with a 105-foot beam. Railroad owners to date included the C&NW, UP, WC, and Canadian National.

The last timber C&NW ore dock at Ashland, Wis., was No. 3 dock, located to the left of No. 2 dock. The dock was 2,040 feet (chute to chute) long and 73 feet high. After 1957 the C&NW operated over the Wisconsin Central (Soo Line) dock until C&NW ceased ore operations here by 1962. Note the foundation for the old No. 1 dock at lower right. The C&NW's Ashland ore dock facility was once the third-largest on the Great Lakes. (Joel Nagro Collection)

The Escanaba timber ore docks were also classic structures. These two docks were the last ones operated by the C&NW—No. 5 is to the left while No. 6 is to the right. (Author's Collection)

An eastbound 46-car loaded ore train moves through Florence, Wisconsin, en route to Escanaba on C&NW's Peninsula Division on July 31, 1948. The train consists of ore loads from the Iron River area, more cars will be added near Iron Mountain before heading for Escanaba. Milwaukee Road 2-8-2 No. 330 was part of the motive power pool shared by the C&NW and the Milwaukee Road for their ore line operations. (Paterson-George Collection)

The low-level dock can unload and handle iron ore pellets for storage on a year-round basis. The facility, known as the Escanaba Ore Terminal, can handle over ten million tons of ore or pellets per year, and has an expansion capability to handle more than 20 million tons annually. The operations in the terminal are completely integrated, with rotary car-dumping equipment, a storage area, and highly mechanized stacking and reclaiming equipment. The entire facility including the ore dock is interconnected with an electrically powered system of conveyors.

Ore trains for the Escanaba operation have varied substantially over the years. The C&NW operated wooden ore cars until the early 1900s, when the first steel cars were placed in operation. The capacity of these original steel cars was 50 tons. By the mid-1920s, the company was purchasing 70-ton ore cars from Pullman and other car builders. The wooden cars were rapidly phased out by the C&NW, and the steel cars became standard operating procedure early in the century.

Originally, the ore trains were scheduled out of Escanaba to both Ishpeming on the Marquette Range, and to a variety of points on the Menominee Range. The trains were carded as third class operations in both directions. Such schedules for ore trains continued until the 1940s, although by then not as extensive as they had been during the early 1900s.

Before getting too far ahead, it is interesting to note that the C&NW exclusively served the Marquette Iron Range at the very beginning of operations during the Civil War.

Later, by 1900, both the Lake Superior & Ishpeming and the Duluth, South Shore & Atlantic railways had taken over the major share of the ore traffic from the Marquette Range. In

During the late 1940s and 1950s, the C&NW and Milwaukee Road operated F-units in their pooled ore service. (Author's Collection)

After its F-units were converted for commuter service the C&NW's ore lines motive power included Fairbanks-Morse 1600-hp road switchers. This train of iron ore pellets is en route from the Groveland Mine north of Iron Mountain to Escanaba. The train traveled over Milwaukee Road trackage from the mine and pelletizing plant to Antoine. From there eastward, the trains operated over C&NW. (Robert C. Anderson)

this case, the the LS&I and the DSS&A moved ore to the ore docks on Lake Superior at Marquette.

Consequently, the C&NW operated but two ore trains in each direction between Escanaba and Ishpeming on a daily-except-Sunday basis. Peninsula Division timetables issued during the early 1900s listed the Ishpeming Ore Freights as Nos. 51 and 53 northbound, and Nos. 52 and 54 southbound. The trains were scheduled for approximately five or six hours each way.

Eventually, with declining traffic and more widespread use of the 70-ton ore car, the C&NW served the Marquette Range with one ore extra (round trip) per day until the early 1970s. From that time on, business began to improve substantially.

Business for the Escanaba ore dock began to improve after the construction of the new low-level ore dock. Instead of simply one ore extra per day, the new traffic began to dictate additional trains. With the expansion of the various mines and pelletizing plants on the Marquette Range including the new and larger Empire Mine, the C&NW found itself running up to five ore extras per day out of Escanaba. Not all of the trains traveled to Ishpeming. Some turned off the Partridge Subdivision at Palmer Junction (south of Negaunee) for the Empire and Tilden Mines. A small yard near the Empire Mine held the loads awaiting shipment to the ore dock. As far as trains running directly into Ishpeming, the number could vary from one to three during any 24-hour period during the 1970s and early 1980s. All ore trains into Ishpeming were switched by the LS&I for the Humboldt, Republic, and other mines in the immediately Negaunee/Eagle Mills area. The LS&I returned the loads to the C&NW's Euclid Yard, which was located on the joint C&NW-LS&I-Soo Line main line (in 2003, this is CN and LS&I trackage).

Despite mine and pellet plant closings, the C&NW maintained the highest traffic level of at least four ore turns per day between Escanaba and Palmer right through the UP merger and the subsequent WC purchase.

On the other hand, one could not say the same thing for the C&NW on the Menominee Range. This particular area covers the Iron Mountain-Iron River-Crystal Falls region, and was once the C&NW's primary ore-hauling operation. Operations were once very extensive—during the early 1900s, the railroad dispatched eight daily-except-Sunday trains out of Escanaba for the Menominee Range. Again, Peninsula Division timetables of the early 1900s indicate that the

trains were operated as third-class. Train operations to the Menominee were much more complex than the Marquette Range operations.

The traffic levels mentioned here were fairly consistent throughout the 1920s. However, the Great Depression caused the bottom to drop out of the ore business during the 1930s. The C&NW and the Milwaukee Road entered into a pooling agreement to reduce expenses and improve services for the Menominee Range mines. From that time on, C&NW ore trains were always a mixture of C&NW and Milwaukee Road ore cars and motive power. This pooling arrangement continued until all but one mine and pelletizing plant remained, the Groveland Mine at Randville, located north of Iron Mountain on the Milwaukee Road. The Milwaukee Road sold its section of railroad to the Escanaba & Lake Superior Railroad in 1980. The E&LS continued to serve the Groveland mine and plant until the facility's closure in 1982.

During the 1940s and 1950s, the C&NW and the Milwaukee Road had an appealing mixture of motive power and equipment. Steam was replaced by diesel power, and at the same time, mine after mine closed on the Menominee Range. Historically, there could be as many six ore turns out of Escanaba during the 1940s, dropping to four and finally two by the early 1960s. One of the trains operated to Iron Mountain, while the other continued through to Stambaugh near Iron River.

Ore traffic declined to just one train per day by the end of the 1970s, with this single run serving the Groveland Mine. The C&NW delivered the train to the Milwaukee Road at Iron Mountain. The Milwaukee Road crew would deliver the empties and bring back loads for the C&NW, which returned the train to Escanaba. The single train usually consisted of about 100 C&NW cars. Since the pooling agreement was all but gone, the Milwaukee Road no longer contributed any ore cars for the operation.

Even though the ore business on the Menominee Range steadily declined throughout the 1950s and 1960s, the C&NW often handled additional ore trains over the line through Iron Mountain and Iron River. Beginning in 1948, the company handled about one million tons annually of Gogebic Range ores (from the Ironwood, Michigan, area) to the Escanaba ore docks. This meant at least one, and sometimes two, empty trains dispatched out of Escanaba every day. The trains ran directly to the Ironwood area and returned to Escanaba. This added substantial tonnage and traffic to the railroad between Iron River and Ironwood (through Watersmeet), which usually never saw much more than some pulpwood traffic.

Over the years, however, this traffic dwindled until there was virtually no business whatsoever. Things were to change for a short while when the C&NW lowered the rates from Ironwood to Escanaba and transferred its ore operations from Ashland to Escanaba in 1960. This produced another trainload of ore to Escanaba on a daily basis, and sometimes two. Counting the empty movements, the C&NW was running from two to four ore trains per day over the line between Escanaba, Iron River, and Ironwood. Add the Iron River trains, and the trains to Iron Mountain during the early 1960s, and the C&NW was dispatching at least four empty trains, and sometimes five or six, to the mining areas. This meant a grand total of eight to twelve trains on the road. All of the trains operated as extras with no timetable authority. The early 1960s saw the last heavy movement of train traffic to and/or through the Menominee Range. By 1967, the Gogebic Range was finished. If it had not been for the Marquette Range picking up in traffic levels, the C&NW's ore operations would have been finished.

Motive Power Notes

During the days of steam, the C&NW operated 2-8-2s and 2-8-0s for train and dock service. Toward the end of steam, one or two 2-8-4s were sent to the ore country. With dieselization, Electro-Motive Division F3s and F7s provided the power for a number of years until their transfer to Chicago-area commuter passenger service in the late 1950s and 1960s. From that time on, Fairbanks-Morse H16-66 "Baby Trainmasters" took over although they were no strangers to the ore country. During the late 1970s, the F-M's were replaced by Alco Century 628s (from the Norfolk & Western), which handled the job until replaced by SD50s and other late-model power from the C&NW and Union Pacific.

Escanaba Terminal Operations

The C&NW's Escanaba terminal operations were unique to the entire Lake Superior/Huron iron ore mining region. Once the 100-car (plus or minus) trains arrived at the ore terminal, a switch crew positioned the train, or parts of it, at the unloading facility. The C&NW trains were automatically positioned and unloaded, three cars at a time, by the operation of a 150-foot mechanical train positioner and a 72-foot tandem rotary car dumper. From the unloading point, pelletized or

unprocessed iron ore moved over a 3,000-foot conveyor belt to the automatic shiploader on the ore dock or to the stockpile area. The shiploader could load ore boats on either side of the dock at the rate of 6,800 tons per hour. The ore cars were weighed automatically just before unloading and all ore was weighed by automatic conveyor scales before loading into vessels.

In the ore storage area, a conveyor led directly to a mechanical stacker which deposited ore or pellets into huge piles 50 feet high, 225 feet wide and as much as 2,500 feet long. A giant multi-bucket excavating machine operated in the storage area to transfer ore to the conveyors moving to the dock for vessel loading. These same basic operations continue in 2003.

The port of Escanaba is in a very advantageous position on Lake Michigan. With the pellet

top: C&NW No. 1561 is a Baldwin AS-616 rebuilt with an EMD hood and 16-567C engine. There were two such C&NW units rebuilt by EMD—the other was No. 1560. When this photograph was taken in June 1970, the unit was assigned to mine transfer duty at Iron Mountain. (Author)

middle: A late-1970s ore extra departs Ishpeming bound for Escanaba powered by two Alco C-630s and one of the rebuilt Baldwins. (Author)

bottom: The C&NW purchased 30 Alco C-628 units from the Norfolk & Western in 1973. By 1975, many had been sent to the ore country to replace older F-M units. No. 6707 and its partners were resting between ore runs at Ishpeming, Michigan. (Author)

63

and ore shipments from both the Marquette and Mesabi Ranges, it appears that the Escanaba Ore Terminal will be around for quite some time well into the 21st century.

The Gogebic Iron Range

The Gogebic Range train operations were just as exciting as those one the Menominee and Marquette Ranges. The C&NW was an active participant in the ore dock operations at Ashland, Wisconsin, for the Gogebic Range ores from 1885 through 1962, the last season of shipping for the company.

The Milwaukee, Lake Shore & Western Railway completed the laying of track between Hurley, Wisconsin, and Ashland in 1885. The new line was opened for traffic on June 1, 1885, but iron ore traffic did not begin until all of the branchline trackage had been built to the mines in the Ironwood (Mich.) area. These projects were completed around October 1, 1885. The company at the same time began construction of the No. 1 ore dock as well as the ore dock yard in Ashland. The latter covered about 40 acres.

The first ore dock built was 1,400 feet long (chute-to-chute length), 46 feet wide, and 40 feet high. The capacity of this dock was 26,000 tons in 234 pockets (117 to a side). A second ore dock had been built to the same specifications by 1888.

above: C&NW 121157 was one of sixty 70-ton ore cars leased from the DM&IR in the 1960s.

right: CNW 122535R in the red scheme.

CNW purchased a number of 70-ton cars from the Lake Superior & Ishpeming. They lacked a lip at the top and had outside bracing on the extension.

middle: A string of ore cars at Ishpeming with pellets from the plant at Republic.

middle right and bottom: Rolling stock use on latter-day all-rail ore movements consisted of C&NW, UP, and MP 100-ton capacity hopper cars. (All, Author)

64

The C&NW took over the MLS&W in 1893, and with the ore traffic growing, the company rebuilt both docks extensively. Eventually a third ore dock was added making the facility one of the most extensive on Lake Superior although it was not quite as big as the Great Northern's in Superior.

Unfortunately, surviving records of ore dock construction on the C&NW in Ashland are incomplete. It is known that during the 1920s there were three ore docks. These three docks were remodeled extensively and were much larger than the original structures.

The No. 1 ore dock was rebuilt in 1916 to a probable length of 1,740 feet. The No. 1 dock was destroyed by fire and dismantled in 1936.

The Nos. 2 and 3 ore docks were identical in length and capacity. Records indicated that they had 340 pockets, were 2,040 feet long and 72 feet high. The No. 2 dock was dismantled in 1948. The No. 3 dock was partially rebuilt during the winter of 1956-57, but was not operated during the shipping season of 1957. The C&NW began shipping ore over the Wisconsin Central ore dock (Soo Line). The No. 3 dock was dismantled in 1960, its last season of service having been 1956.

The C&NW operated over the Soo Line ore dock rather extensively. From 1948 through 1953, the C&NW leased 60 pockets and operated on the ore dock during the midnight shift. The Soo and the C&NW jointly operated the ore dock from 1957 through 1962. The Soo ore dock has not been used since 1965.

Ore production in the Ironwood area peaked in the early 1920s when nearly seven million tons were shipped through the C&NW docks at Ashland. From then on production declined with various ups and downs over the years until nothing was shipped in 1966. The Gogebic Range was in a complete shutdown by 1968. The C&NW's ore operations ceased in 1962. From that time on, all iron ore production at mines served by the C&NW went east through the Escanaba docks.

Just as the C&NW pooled ore operations on the Menominee Range, so it did with the Soo Line on the Gogebic Range. On March 26, 1934, the company established an agreement that the C&NW would handle 69 percent, and the Soo 31 percent, of all the ore mined and shipped through the port of Ashland. The railroads operated over each other's trackage between Hoyt, Wisconsin, and Wakefield, Michigan. For many years, they pooled their cars but from 1956 on the

equipment remained with its owners only. Until 1950 the equipment consisted of 50-ton capacity ore cars only. After that time, the C&NW began purchasing additional 70-ton ore cars and this equipment began showing up in Ashland on the C&NW only. The Soo Line could not operate the larger equipment because of clearance problems at some of the mines (including the Montreal and the Carey) on their trackage.

For many years the C&NW scheduled the Gogebic Range ore trains between Ashland and Orva, an ore train assembly yard west of Hurley. Seven scheduled third-class trains were dispatched out of Ashland on a daily basis for the ore business. Early in the 20th century, the ore trains were scheduled both ways. By the 1930s, the company scheduled only the empty eastbound movements. This philosophy continued through the late 1940s. Beyond that time, all of the ore trains were operated as "extras."

Not all eastbound empty ore trains terminated at Orva. Some operated beyond Hurley and Ironwood to set out empties for the mine run transfers operating to and from the Wakefield area.

From the late 1940s on, ore train traffic began to decline. From seven turns per day, it was down to three and four turns by the early 1950s. Dieselization was part of the change because train size could increase from 80 cars to 150 for a three-unit F7 consist.

By 1957, the C&NW was operating only one or two ore extras per day between Ashland and the Ironwood area. Orva, by then, was no longer used as a yard. With three- and four-unit combinations, train size had grown to over 175 cars, and 200-car trains were not unheard of. The ore trains were a mixture of 50- and 70-ton ore cars.

The ore business had declined to the point of one ore extra per day to and from Ironwood by 1959. Although the train was still long, this too would change by 1961 with the single train running with two 1600-hp Fairbank-Morse road switchers and eighty 50-ton ore cars. After 1960, the C&NW sent all of the 70-ton cars to the Escanaba operations, and only 50-ton cars remained for the declining Gogebic Range services. By 1962, ore traffic had declined to virtually nothing and after that season, the company ceased operating any ore trains out of the port of Ashland.

Motive power for the Gogebic Range operations consisted of 4-6-0 Ten Wheelers and 2-8-0 Consolidations for the mine run transfers, 2-8-2 Mikados for the road operations, and 4-6-0s for the ore yard and dock operations in Ashland. The latter were among the smallest steam power used for ore dock service in modern times. After dieselization, road switchers of all types were operated in mine run transfer service, while the F7s took over the road operations. Later the FM "Baby Trainmasters" held down every job from the ore dock in Ashland, over-the-road hauls, and mine runs. GP9s were also operated on the ore dock in Ashland after 1956, when the company transferred all operations to the Soo Line facility. As mentioned earlier, the C&NW operated Alco 1000-hp switchers on the Ashland docks for a short while in the early 1950s. However, the 4-6-0s continued on a regular basis until January 1957. When the ore season ended in December 1956, the C&NW had 500 cars of frozen ore that had to wait until spring for thawing and dumping on the ore dock. The cars were stored at Ashland for the entire winter. The 4-6-0s in ore service were always stained with the red ores. The yellow diesels were always kept a little cleaner and never did suffer from excessive ore staining, at least in the Ashland operations.

The former DSS&A main line is the only rail line near the Gogebic Range at this writing. The route is now part of the Wisconsin Central Division of the Canadian National Railways.

All-Rail Ore Movements

All-rail movements of ore or pellets from the mines directly to the steel mill centers have been another important aspect of North Western ore operations.

In one case, the company handled about 40 carloads of iron ore per day from the Gogebic Range bound for St. Louis-area mills during the 1950s and 1960s. Train 282, the old time freight out of Ashland, would be assigned four 1600-hp "Baby Trainmasters." No. 282 would pick up the 40 cars at Hurley and take them south. Through connections with the L&M, the C&NW handled the ore all the way from Michigan to southern Illinois.

Iron ore and/or pellets were also shipped out of Upper Michigan to various steel company destinations. In some cases, the C&NW did the entire haul from the Ishpeming area to Chicago or even St. Louis. In other cases, the Milwaukee Road interchanged trainloads of ore with the C&NW at Proviso Yard in Chicago. The C&NW then operated the train to the St. Louis area.

The C&NW did handle one regular year-round operation of all-rail ore. In this case, the Inland Steel Company iron ore pellet plant at

Black River Falls, Wisconsin, shipped about one million tons annually to its Indiana Harbor Works in East Chicago, Indiana. The C&NW handled the ore in 100-ton capacity ore cars directly to the Chicago area. The ore was interchanged with the Indiana Harbor Belt Railroad for delivery to the steel mill. The mine and plant closed in 1983 and was the last ore operation in the state of Wisconsin.

Still another all-rail operation was primarily a winter season operation, but not exclusively. In this case, U.S. Steel shipped trainloads of pellets over the C&NW between Superior and Chicago-area interchanges. The Duluth, Missabe & Iron Range Railway handled the 100-car trains to South Itasca, where the C&NW picked up the train. Before departure, the train was inspected and the power was coupled on. In addition, a two-unit helper was coupled to the rear of the train. For 16 miles the helper engines pushed until the top of the hill was reached at Hawthorne. This is the range of hills that virtually completely circles Lake Superior, especially on the western end. (The grades are even tougher in Minnesota.) The all-rail trains once operated via Spooner and Hudson, Wisconsin, before continuing toward Chicago. The empty trains operated on a more direct route via Bloomer, Wisconsin. This operation continued until a bridge between Spooner and Eau Claire was reconstructed to handle the short, heavy ore cars.

Ore traffic out of Superior during winter was sometimes so heavy as to merit four loaded trains southward during a single 24-hour period. Not all of the ore trains went to the Chicago or St. Louis areas. Since the early 1980s, all-rail trains have been operating to Provo, Utah. The C&NW handled the trains at first via Eau Claire, and then west to the Twin Cities and south to the UP connection at Omaha. Later, the company began operating the trains out of Superior over the Burlington Northern to the Twin Cities region.

The consist of the Utah trains included 100-ton cars from the C&NW, Missouri Pacific, and the Union Pacific. After the UP merger with the Southern Pacific, SP and Rio Grande cars were part of these all-rail trains.

After unloading the taconite pellets, the empty trains return to Wyoming where they are loaded with coal for movement to Wisconsin power plants. Once emptied, the trains return to Superior and the connection with the DM&IR for movement to the Minntac Plant, and the cycle begins again with a two-way loaded operation—a two-way win.

facing page: With C&NW SD40-2 No. 6860 "on the point" of a five-unit power consist (including three from Union Pacific), an all-rail ore train bound for Provo, Utah, moves on the Burlington Northern main line at Saunders. This was in the days when cabooses still punctuated the end of the train—a classic yellow C&NW bay window car brings up the rear. (All, Author)

A quick side bar: The C&NW tracks have been abandoned south of Superior to Rice Lake. Thus all ex-C&NW, Union Pacific trains operate over the Wisconsin Central between Superior and Necedah, Wisconsin, where the WC route connects with the ex-C&NW main line between Chicago and the Twin Cities.

Ore on the Omaha Road

Before closing this chapter, we must take a look at the Omaha Road ore operation out of Ashland. The Zenith Furnace Company in Duluth purchased the high-grade ores from the Gogebic Range. The ore arrived in Ashland in the regular ore trains, or in some cases, in time freight 281. The ore was transferred from the ore yard to the Omaha's yard on the west side of Ashland. Since the trackage between Ashland and Spooner was so light, with light bridge capacities, the Omaha crews would separate each ore load with an empty box car. It was an expensive way to move ore, especially since the company had to move it to Spooner and then back up to Superior and interchange it with the Northern Pacific for delivery. The distance traveled between Ashland, Spooner, and Duluth was 155 miles. Compare that distance with the direct route via the Northern Pacific of just 75 miles. The extra mileage and the extra switching of the box cars, both in and out of the ore car consists could not have made this a profitable movement for the C&NW. It is interesting to note, however, that the movement existed for at least 20 or 30 years. The Zenith Furnace Company purchased the Gogebic Range ores because of their high quality as compared to the Mesabi ores, which had a slightly lower iron content—in fact, up to ten percentage points lower. Many Gogebic ores were over 65 percent iron, the same as many of the pellets produced in plants on both the Mesabi and Marquette Ranges. The Zenith Furnace Company went out of business years ago, and thus no Michigan ores are sent westward for that company's furnaces. Besides that, all of the trackage between Ashland and Superior on the former NP and Omaha has been torn up.

The C&NW did a superb job of handling iron ore from the three Michigan ranges, as well as the Mesabi all-rail movements. The ore business was a major part of the North Western's traffic mix. As we look at the Union Pacific today, the all-rail routes to Chicago and Utah are still part of the ex-C&NW traffic mix—part of the C&NW ore history continues to live on as we move deeper into the 21st century.

6

Black Diamonds

When one mentions the Chicago & North Western Railway, coal trains are not the first thing that comes to mind. Commuter streamliners, *400s*, *Falcons*, and ore trains, perhaps, but not necessarily coal trains. However, the C&NW was a major coal hauler and had been since about 1914 when tracks were laid to the southern Illinois coal fields and a connection made with the Macoupin County Railway.

Southern Illinois Coal

Actually the Macoupin County Railway was the first line, as far as the C&NW system was concerned, to be built for the specific purpose of serving coal mines. The MC was built in 1904 between Girard and Benld, a distance of about 24 miles.

The C&NW reached the southern Illinois fields through a series of constructions that began in 1901. During that year, the Peoria & North-

Western Railway constructed 83 miles of track between Nelson and Peoria. Further progress was not made until 1913 and 1914 when the St. Louis, Peoria & North Western Railway completed 91 miles of line between Peoria and Girard via Pekin, Illinois.

The C&NW built these segments of line to reach a number of coal mines around Benld that the company had purchased for their own locomotive fuel. In order to complete the connection to the mines, the Macoupin County Extension Railway built four more miles of railroad between Staunton and Benld in 1914. From that time, coal trains were a way of life for what was known for many years as the Southern District of the former Galena Division. Prior to 1939 the line was known as the Southern Illinois Division.

Construction and expansion, however, ended for this District in 1914. In 1927 the C&NW

completed another 2-1/2 miles of railroad from Staunton to DeCamp, Ill., for a connection with Litchfield & Madison Railway. Although the trackage was built by the C&NW, the L&M actually operated the line between DeCamp and Benld to ferry the time freight to and from St. Louis. However, there were also coal mines on the L&M, which fed traffic on to the C&NW.

During the days of steam on the "Old S.I."— as the territory was sometimes called—Ten-Wheelers and Consolidations handled the classification of coal at Benld and South Pekin as well as the mine-run transfers to various mines around Benld. Prior to the C&NW's absorption of the Minneapolis & St. Louis Railway, a pool arrangement for crew assignments was set up for the mine at Middle Grove. Middle Grove is located about 25 miles west of Peoria on what was the main line of the M&StL. All of this coal fed into the

Triple-headers were not uncommon on the C&NW's Southern Illinois coal trains in the days of steam. Berkshire No. 2810 is leading a northbound train, which includes some general freight behind the first block of loaded coal cars. (C&NW Railway Photo, Author's Collection)

north toward Nelson and Chicago. Sometimes the coal was reclassified at South Pekin.

Dieselization occured in 1948 in the form of Electro-Motive Division F3s and sometimes the FTs, the first road freight power purchased by the C&NW. By 1950 and 1951, however, the company was sending three-unit F7s to handle the 150-car coal trains, which weighed over 11,000 tons. As in the days of steam, Radnor Hill (north of South Pekin) required helpers. Consequently, the C&NW assigned a three-unit helper to all northbound coal trains out of South Pekin. Even with 9,000 horsepower, it was no picnic taking a ten- or 12-thousand ton train over the hill. It is interesting to note that a J-4 Berkshire with a helper could only handle 5,500 tons up the hill.

Coal trains during the 1980s from the Benld area and the Elm Mine were still very much a part of the traffic mix between Benld and Nelson, the junction with the Chicago–Omaha main line. Coal also moved south toward St. Louis. Virtually all of the coal was en route to electric generating plants. Furthermore, the heavy coal traffic was no longer confined to the "S.I." during this period.

Beginning in the late 1950s, the C&NW began to interchange unit coal trains with the Illinois Central for the Oak Creek Electric generating plant near Milwaukee. This added a segment of C&NW trackage to these heavy coal movements.

Moving into the 1980s, the C&NW also handled coal from the Louisville & Nashville Railroad for the Oak Creek plant. Another coal train operated over the main line from Fremont (the new Union Pacific connection bypassing Omaha) to Nelson, Illinois, and then south to Peoria for a connection with the Chicago & Illinois Midland Railroad for eventual delivery at Havanna, Illinois. With the Wyoming coal trains moving south over the old S.I. , one could find loaded coal trains rolling in both directions over what was the South Pekin Subdivision of the C&NW's Illinois Division.

The C&NW had other coal operations which did not involve mining operations. The railroad served coal docks in Milwaukee, Green Bay, Escanaba, and Ashland for nearly a century. Some of this service resulted in some rather extensive operations. Coal was transloaded from boats to rail cars for delivery to various cities and small towns for home heating and electric generating plants. Eventually these small operations all but disappeared. Many of the small electric generating plants turned to oil and natural gas when it was believed that the world had an unlimited and inexpensive supply of both commodities. Many of

C&NW. In fact, mining operations continued at the Elm Mine and the C&NW continued to serve the company. The Elm Mine at Middle Grove was located at the end of the Elm Subdivision. Ultimately the line became part of the Elm Industrial Lead extending from Molitor Junction on the Peoria Sub to Elm Grove, a distance of 23.9 miles. The entire lead was out of service by the mid-1990s.

For road power, the C&NW operated class J Mikados until the arrival of the 12 class J-4 Berkshire 2-8-4s, built by Alco in 1927. These Super Power, low-drivered engines were constructed specifically for the coal train operations to and from southern Illinois.

The mine-run transfers brought the coal to the yards mentioned previously. Yard crews assembled the coal trains as solid units, or placed the loads as fill on the various time freights operating

top: Class Z, 2-8-0 steam power was operated for yard switching at South Pekin, Illinois until dieselization. No. 1800 was photographed on April 27, 1947. (Paul Stringham, Author's Collection)

middle: Another example of steam power used on the C&NW's Southern Illinois coal line were the Class J, 2-8-2s, such as No. 2524 at the South Adams Street Yard in Peoria in August, 1947. (Paul Stringham, Author's Collection)

below: C&NW Extra 1771 West is a Middle Grove mine coal turn on the Minneapolis & St. Louis Railroad's trackage at Kickapoo Creek, just west of Peoria, Illinois. (Paul Stringham, Author's Collection)

The arrival of later model diesels, such as EMD F7s, bumped earlier FT's and F3s to southern Illinois coal trains. Here No. 4051 conquers Radnor Hill just north of Peoria on July 19, 1951. (Paul Stringham; William S. Kuba Collection)

Coal hopper No. 60711 (60001-60999 series, odd numbers only) was rebuilt in 1947 and painted box car red with white lettering. (C&NW Historical Society)

the coal docks on Lake Michigan and Superior were closed, and naturally the traffic dwindled substantially.

The coal docks in Ashland and Superior shipped coal as far west as South Dakota with the C&NW and subsidiary Omaha Road handling the traffic. Although solid coal trains were not the order of the day, there were anywhere from five- to 30-car blocks of coal going west every day during the winter season. Imagine, if you will, the Omaha freight departing Ashland for Spooner with one or two Geeps or Fairbanks-Morse road switchers (or a classic piece of steam power), handling regular freight plus one or more blocks of Omaha and C&NW 50- and 70-ton coal hoppers. This added a healthy percentage of revenue for the route between Ashland and the Twin Cities via Spooner. With the coal traffic down to nothing for many years, the line between Hayward and Ashland Junction was eventually abandoned in the late 1970s. The tracks were taken up by 1979.

Since the C&NW constructed the lines to Southern Illinois, the size of equipment has grown from the 40-ton capacity wooden and steel cars to the 50-, 70-, 90-, and eventually 100-ton capacity cars. The C&NW owned an extensive fleet of coal hoppers. Furthermore, it was involved with the operation of equipment through interchange including cars of electric generating company ownership, the Union Pacific, Burlington Northern, Illinois Central, Louisville & Nashville, and the Chicago & Eastern Illinois. (In fact, it was not unusual to see IC, L&N, and C&EI coal hoppers in all-rail iron ore service.) Interestingly enough, motive power and cabooses were all interchanged on the through unit-train runs. Consequently, coal train consists on the C&NW

Another group of C&NW 70-ton hopper cars included No. 64247 (64001-65003, odd numbers only), which was built by Pullman-Standard in 1940. The quad hopper was originally painted box car red with white lettering including the full Chicago & North Western name and herald. Note the word "Line" in the herald as opposed to the word "System" on car No. 60711 (facing page), which had been rebuilt in 1947. (C&NW Historical Society)

above: Off-set side, 70 ton triple hopper No. 65215 (65101-68103, odd numbers) was built in 1945 by Pullman-Standard. By 1945, C&NW had ceased lettering this equipment with the full name. This group of hoppers served systemwide from southern Illinois to northern Wisconsin and the far west. (C&NW Historical Society)

middle left: Car 65629 was part of the 65101-68103 series. (Author)

middle right: Quad hopper No. 76549 was part of series 75801-76799 (odd numbers only). The car was built in 1937 and rebuilt in 1955. Additional work was done on the car at Green Bay in 1965. It was painted red oxide when photographed in the 1970s. (Author)

bottom: Coal movements from coal docks on the Great Lakes—such as at Ashland, Superior, and Duluth—were handled in regular time freights and locals. One can see two sets of coal hoppers within this freight train. (C&NW Historical Society)

74

displayed a wide variety of equipment and owner-ship from the 1940s and 1950s through to the Union Pacific merger in 1995.

The Powder River Basin

During the 1950s, when many firms were switching from coal to oil and natural gas, there were many forecasts that the coal industry would be gone by the 21st century, with the possible exception of metallurgical coal for the steel industry. No one would have imagined the impact that non-sulphur coal would have on the railroad industry beginning in the 1960s.

Among the C&NW's coal traffic developments in the 1960s was the receiving of unit coal trains from Wyoming coal fields via the Union Pacific at Council Bluffs. Some of these trains were destined for the Oak Creek facility while others were interchanged with the Illinois Central at Chicago.

While the Great Northern and Northern Pacific were working to establish through coal train services from Montana to Minnesota Power in 1968, the C&NW was eyeing the possibility of such traffic. While the North Western was engaged in other coal traffic operations, the western coal held a whole new concept in long-distance train services.

As the North Western moved through the 1970s, plans were formulated for building a new coal line in Wyoming as well as a new working relationship with the Burlington Northern for western coal traffic.

The C&NW and the new Burlington Northern began talking about what could be done and informed the ICC they had reached in agreement in principle to jointly build and operate a 100-mile line in Wyoming's Powder River Basin in mid-1975. The two railroads had already filed requests for ICC approval to build separate lines. However, the ICC was in favor of a joint line to minimize impact on the environment while at the same time speeding up relief for Amerca's energy shortage. The new C&NW-BN line would open up new opportunities for access to low-sulfur coal deposits.

The ICC approved the BN-C&NW coal line contract by mid-1976. The contract was amended permitting the BN to move ahead with construction while the C&NW worked out arrangements to finance its share of the building costs. This would end up taking the C&NW a bit longer than it originally anticipated, and it had to come up with some creative ideas. The C&NW began working out a plan with the Union Pacific in 1978.

The two railroad companies announced their new plan in December 1978. The C&NW proposed that it would build a line about 80 miles long to link the C&NW with the UP for hauling coal for Eastern and Southwestern markets. The new connection would be part of the new multi-railroad route for low-sulfur coal from the Powder River Basin, and would also serve as an alternate to a rebuilt C&NW main line across most of Nebraska.

The C&NW modified its loan application, which turned out to be substantially less than what would have been required for the joint financing of the 100-mile line with the BN, and the rebuilding of 500 miles of C&NW line in Nebraska and Wyoming. Things were set in place for the C&NW to build the new connection with the UP from a point east of Shawnee, Wyoming, where the new BN-C&NW coal line met the C&NW main line and southeast to the UP's main line. The C&NW would deliver the coal trains to the UP, who in turn would deliver them to connections at or near Omaha to the C&NW as well as to the Missouri Pacific and other railroad lines

It took awhile for things to fall into place. Finally, in late in 1983, the troubles came to an end. *Railway Age* carried a short article in its

Western coal traffic has played a major role in the C&NW's freight services. Two C&NW units, Nos. 928 and 927, lead two Union Pacific units, one of which is a GP9 "B" unit. The train is slowly moving through the coal loader at the mine at Reliance, Wyoming, on May 2, 1971. After loading, the train will head east for delivery to an electric power plant. (William S. Kuba)

December 1983 issue with the title, "99-Year Pact Ends BN-C&NW Quarrel." BN and C&NW signed two agreements covering costs and operations, and litigation between the two railroads was dropped. The C&NW obtained a 50 percent interest in 93 miles of railroad, part of the BN-built Orin–Gillette line which had been completed in 1979. The C&NW completed rebuilding 45 miles of main line in Wyoming and the 56-mile connecting line to the Union Pacific at Joyce, Nebraska, in 1984. Powder River coal began moving in late 1984.

The new long-haul coal operations began to cover a wide variety of destinations. Not only did the coal move over the Overland Route to Chicago, but also to various generating plants on the C&NW system. Eventually, the C&NW delivered coal trains to the Wisconsin Central (now part of Canadian National) at Minneapolis for delivery to Green Bay, Wisconsin. Coal trains were also sent to Superior, Wisconsin, for transloading to Great Lakes ships for delivery to Marquette, Michigan, and Detroit Edison. This system of unit train operations over the line to Chicago, the Twin Cities, and elsewhere continues with the Union Pacific in 2003.

By 1990, annual coal tonnage over the C&NW hit the 22-million mark. This is substantially different from 1965 when the company handled one million plus tons of coal prior to the new western coal traffic. There is no doubt about it—the C&NW, long known as a Granger Road, also fit the description of a Coal Road!

left: This Wisconsin Power & Light unit coal train is pausing at the Beverly Yard in Cedar Rapids, Iowa, on July 21, 1979. Although Union Pacific power was quite common, this particular train is led by C&NW SD45 No. 958, followed by Burlington Northern 5532 and three Milwaukee Road General Electrics. (William S. Kuba)

below: Two eastbound coal trains are lined up to roll at South Morrill, Nebraska, on July 24, 1987. (Lou Schmitz)

top: Coal hopper No. 63048 (63000 to 63164 series) was a 100-ton car built by Bethlehem Steel in 1966 and designated "Unit Train Service Only." (Bethlehem Steel; Author's Collection)

middle: C&NW 63575 was part of the 63500-63699 series, painted black with white lettering. This 100-ton car was actually owned by the Alton & Southern. (Lou Schmitz)

below: With No. 7011 leading, a westbound empty coal train travels over the former Omaha Road trackage at Kasota, Minnesota, (just north of Mankato) on October 28, 1986. The prefered route for the coal train traffic to and from northern Minnesota and Wisconsin power plants was through Mason City on the "Spine Line," formerly Rock Island trackage. (William S. Kuba)

above: With GE DASH8-40C No. 8514 doing the honors on the head end, a C&NW coal train heads east at Logan, Wyoming, on September 3, 1981. (Lou Schmitz)

left: The Overland Route between the Missouri Valley and Chicago is one of the primary lines for the heavy duty long-haul Western coal traffic. This photo illustrates a typical train equipped with aluminum coal cars heading east near Bertram, Iowa, on July 23, 1984. The GE power will soon be down to a crawl as the train tackles Vernon Hill. (William S. Kuba)

Freight Equipment

7

This chapter is a review of part of the C&NW freight car fleet, especially over the time period when many of the freight cars carried reporting marks for North Western subsidiaries Omaha Road (CMO), Minneapolis & St. Louis (M&StL), Chicago Great Western (CGW), and others over the past half century. The C&NW's ore cars and coal-hauling equipment are covered in Chapters 5 and 6.

The freight car fleet is a crucial part of any railroad's tools for providing dependable transportation. After all, it is the carload that earns revenue, not locomotive miles.

Freight equipment is also a rolling advertisement for the railroad company. Not only are the cars visible to the public eye on a daily basis throughout North America, but shippers and receivers take critical note of the condition of equipment in which their freight is handled.

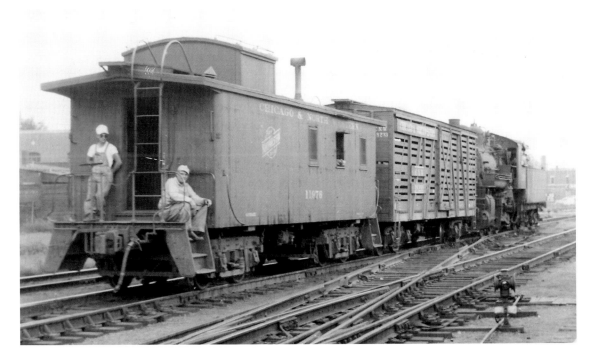

Forty-foot box car 82540 (series 81452-84250) was built in 1945 by General American. It carried slogans for the "Overland Route" and "Route of the *400* Streamliners." (GATC, Author's Collection)

We are in Cedar Rapids in August, 1953, and steam is still the primary power for switching on many parts of the C&NW. Stock car 18233 (series 18001-18999, odd numbers only) is ahead of the caboose on this switch run powered by 0-6-0 No. 2148. (William S. Kuba)

Series 49800-49998 (even numbers only) was built in 1929, and there were still 13 of the 40-foot double-door auto box cars left in service in 1956. (GATC Photo, Author's Collection)

Forty-foot PS1 box car 7 (series 1-625) was built in 1953 by Pullman-Standard. The car proudly carried "The Overland Route" adjacent to the "B" (hand brake) end of the car. (C&NW Photo, Author's Collection)

C&NW freight equipment came in all colors including box car red, bright red, yellow, green, black, blue, and combination yellow and green. Lettering has been black, white, green, or yellow depending upon the basic color of the car.

The book *The Chicago and North Western Final Freight Car Roster*, compiled by Joseph Piersen and Ira Kulbersh and published by the Chicago & North Western Historical Society in 1999, is recommended as an excellent review of the entire fleet as it existed at the time of the Union Pacific merger in 1995.

With C&NW's acquisition of the Minneapolis & St. Louis came a group of box cars painted green with gold lettering, such as No. 5076.

M&StL 54734 was refurbished by the C&NW at Clinton in November 1968. The car carried its M&StL reporting marks with a C&NW logo. (Both, Author)

above: Automobile box car 57694 (40-foot, series 57400-57898) was built by P-S in 1948. (C&NW Photo, Author's Collection)

clockwise from far left: Forty-foot box cars 83456, 81298, 71812, and 140026 exhibit paint and lettering changes seen through the years. (All, Author)

below: The C&NW rebuilt a group of 40-foot box cars in 1963. They had been built in 1943 with single-sheathed wood sides to conserve steel during World War II. Cars in rebuilt series 79250-80250 (even numbers) were equipped with 9-foot doors. (C&NW Photo, Author's Collection)

Forty-foot cars in series 32000-32024, were equipped with "DF" (Damage Free) loading devices and a plug door. This car was rebuilt at Clinton in December 1967. (Author)

Fifty-foot box car 4516 (series 4142-4641) was built in 1955 by P-S, and was lettered with a large "C&NW" instead of the "Overland Route" or "400" slogan. These 50-ton capacity box cars were equipped with 8-foot doors. (C&NW Photo, Author's Collection)

When the C&NW acquired the Rock Island's "Spine Line" from the Twin Cities to Kansas City, some former Rock Island freight equipment was given C&NW reporting marks, but often the Rock Island herald was left in place and not painted out. Such was the case with CNW 701935, series 701000 to 702499, photographed in 1988. (Thomas A. Dorin)

Fifty-foot ACF box car 154836 (series 154000-154999), built in 1967 and painted red with yellow lettering, had a cushion underframe. (C&NW Photo, Author's Collection)

P-S exterior-post box car 163163 (series 163000-163299) had 10-foot doors. (Author)

Fifty-foot "waffle-side" cars 160300-161999 were built by P-S in 1969. (C&NW Photo, Author's Collection)

Double-plug-door 60-foot car 91520 was built in 1963 and assigned to auto parts service for the Ford Motor Company. Series 91520-91546 carried the instructions "When empty return to NYC Railroad, Warren, Michigan." (Thrall Photo, Author's Collection)

Double-door auto parts box car 91525 (series 91520-91546) carried stenciled instructions indicating that it was to be returned to the Grand Trunk Western at Flint, Michigan, when empty. (Thrall Photo, Author's Collection)

Car 91314 was built in 1965 by the Thrall Car Manufacturing Company as part of series 91300-91317. The "when empty" instructions on the 91314 designated return movement to the Union Railroad at Irving, Pennsylvania. The car was assigned to GM's Fisher Body. Note the simplified painting arrangement compared to the two cars above, with black having been dropped from the ends and logo. (Thrall Photo, Author's Collection)

CNW
92001
CAPY 100000 XML
LD LMT 110000
LT WT 110000   NEW 8-64

WHEN EMPTY RETURN TO
WABASH R.R BUFFALO, NY

CNW
92094
CAPY 100000 XL
LD LMT 101700
LT WT 118300 NEW 5-67

WHEN EMPTY RETURN TO NYC RR
WARREN, MICH. 88

HYDRAULIC CUSHION

CNW
92044
CAPY   XML
LD LMT
LT WT   NEW 1-65

WHEN EMPTY
RETURN TO B&O
R.R. PARMA,
OHIO

DO NOT LOAD OR
UNLOAD THIS CAR
UNLESS ALL DOORS
ARE OPEN

CLOSE & LOCK
DOORS BEFORE
MOVING CAR

HYDRAULIC CUSHION

far left: Hi-cube car 92001 (92000-92024 series) was assigned to Ford. (Thrall Photo, Author's Collection)

opposite middle: C&NW 92094 was an 86-foot hi-cube car (series 92094-92120) assigned to Chrysler. (Thrall Photo, Author's Collection)

opposite bottom: Car 92044 (series 92025-92047) was assigned to Chevrolet. (Thrall Photo, Author's Collection)

top: North Western Refrigerator Line Company (NWX) 12220 was a wood-sheathed ice refrigerator car with steel ends and roof. Paint was green and yellow. (Author)

second from top: Steel cars like 40-footer 729 eventually became part of the NWX fleet along with the various wood cars. (Author)

left: NWX 12086 was a wood refrigerator car from series 12000-12300. It was photographed at Schiller Park (Chicago), Illinois, on May 30, 1968. (William A. Raia)

bottom: Mechanical refrigerator cars finally replaced the ice-bunker cars from the wooden and steel classes. Car 61075 (series 61000-61099) had CNW reporting marks, was 59 feet, 3 inches long over the coupler faces, and was equipped with an 8-foot plug door. It was painted in the traditional yellow-and-green color scheme. (Author)

CNW 32633 (32616-32702) was a 50-foot insulated box car built in 1965, with a yellow body and black ends and lettering. (GATC, Author's Collection)

C&NW 50-foot insulated plug-door box car 50691. (Author)

Chicago, St. Paul, Minneapolis & Omaha flat car 59673 (series 59601-59999, odd numbers only). (Basgen Photography, Dan Mackey Collection)

top left: M&StL bulkhead flat car No. 16201. (Thomas A. Dorin)

above: Bulkhead flat 48709 (series 48653-48759) was a 56-foot car. (Author)

left: CGW reporting marks on bulkhead flat 3022 (series 3011-3030). (Thomas A. Dorin)

below: Car No. 39600 (series 39600-39649) handled coiled steel shipments. Twin covers protected steel from weather in transit. Colors were yellow and green. (Thrall Photo, Author's Collection)

top: Gondola 89009 (89003-89072) was green with yellow lettering and was photographed at Clinton in 1995. (Joe Piersen)

above: Gondola 129041 (129000-129220) was painted black, and was out of service when photographed in April 1989. (Joe Piersen)

second from bottom: Car 132603 (132600-132799 series) in green at Proviso Yard, Chicago, in June 1989. (Joe Piersen)

bottom: Gondola 340564 (340500-340583 series) was black with white lettering. Shown at Proviso in May 1989. (Joe Piersen)

above: CNW 350187, shown in July 1989, is a former "RailGon" car. The cars were numbered in the 350100-350399 series and were 57 feet, 1 inch long. (Joe Piersen)

left: Gondola 370122 was under a long-term lease to C&NW and was photographed just prior to the UP merger in 1995. (Joe Piersen)

left: Forty-foot, 50-ton capacity high-side gondola 117029 (series 117000-117599) was painted black with white lettering. (Author)

bottom: Two views of 70-ton covered hopper cars from the 95200-95354 series. Cars 95316 and 95329 were painted in a typical covered hopper scheme of gray with black lettering. (Both, Thomas A. Dorin)

top left: Moving to the 100-ton capacity covered hopper cars, CNW 96767 was also painted in the gray scheme.

top right: Covered hopper 96654 received the yellow scheme with a neat lettering arrangement and full-color insignia. Cars in the 65101-68103 series also received a green color scheme.

right: Air Slide car GACX 42015 (42005-42114) was leased by the C&NW from General American. The 40-foot car had a 55-ton capacity.

right: CNW 96402 is a 100-ton capacity grain hopper, part of the 95970-96469 series.

bottom left: CNW 179010 (series 178600-179099) was built in 1980 and painted in the green scheme.

bottom right: Covered hopper 182602 (series 181000-182699), a 60-foot grain car, arrived on the C&NW roster in 1981. (All, Author)

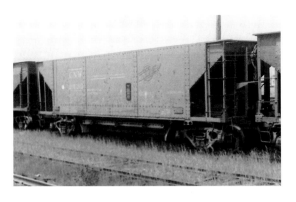

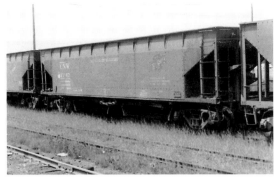

top: Two examples of C&NW ballast cars, often used in revenue service for rock and other bulk or stone traffic. The photos were taken in the early 1970s. The cars were painted box car red with white lettering. (Both, Author)

left: Stock cars 32903 and 36779 in the consist of a time freight at Belle Plaine, Iowa, in November 1954. Most C&NW stock cars wore box car red; the final color scheme was green and yellow. (William S. Kuba)

below: C&NW stock car 15001 (series 15000-15049) was built by the General American Car Company at East Chicago in January 1921. The 36-foot double-deck car served the industry faithfully for decades. (GATC Photo, Author's Collection)

8
Cabooses

The photos on the following pages illustrate a cross-section of the Chicago & North Western's caboose fleet as it existed until the vast majority of cars were taken out of service prior to the Union Pacific merger.

With a few exceptions, most members of the latter-day North Western caboose fleet were bay window cars. There were some interesting second-hand cabooses with center cupolas, as well as cabooses inherited through the C&NW's mergers with the Litchfield & Madison, the Minneapolis & St. Louis, and the Chicago Great Western.

The North Western's final paint scheme for its caboose fleet introduced a very positive image for the railroad. The new program went from the traditional red to a bright yellow and green, with eye-catching slogans promoting safety and the C&NW's employee ownership. It was a super way to end the consist of a freight train.

above: A potash train from the Duluth, Winnipeg & Pacific has been picked up by the C&NW and is running eastward through Superior, Wis., to Itasca Yard in 1984. (Thomas Dorin)

left: Wood-bodied caboose 11768 has had its cupola windows blanked out and is lettered for transfer service at the Chicago yards in this 1970s view. Prior to the arrival of bay window steel cabooses, this type of car was typical of cabooses operating systemwide on the C&NW. (Author)

above: Wood bay window caboose 6110 on a work train in the Chicago Yards in the early 1970s. (Author)

above right: When the Chicago Great Western was absorbed into the C&NW System, the cars continued to carry the CGW reporting marks. With a modified window arrangement, CGW 10517 was designated "Terminal Only Twin Cities." (Author)

right: CGW 10514 in yellow at Kansas City in April 1980 had very tiny "CNW" initials. (Dennis Roos)

four bottom views: Bay window caboose 10385 illustrates part of the rebuilding process with body windows plated over, the "Employee Owned" slogan, and the American flag.

No. 10864 represents a typical C&NW bay window caboose during the last decades of caboose operations for the railroad.

No. 10871 illustrates the slogan "Pulling Together!"

Bay window car 11080 bore the slogan "We Originated Safety First!" (All, Author)

left: Caboose 11226 included the American flag as well as a more detailed slogan, "Since 1848 Pulling Together For Safety and Service."

second from top: Caboose 10927 displayed the slogan, "We're Employee Owned" Ironwood, Mich., in June 1978.

bottom left: Caboose 11194 has a slightly different lettering scheme for the CNW reporting marks and the car number below the window.

bottom right: Widevision caboose 11194 had its cupola windows blanked—along with all but one window on each side of its carbody—to protect crew members and reduce the expense of installing bullet-proof glazing as required by the Federal Railroad Administration (FRA). (All, Author)

9

Union Pacific

It could be said that the year 1995 was a "Red Letter Year" for the Chicago & North Western Railway. With that year's merger of the C&NW into the Union Pacific system, the red letters "Union Pacific" were applied as former North Western motive power was repainted in Union Pacific's classic Armour yellow and Harbor Mist gray scheme.

Freight service retained much of its pre-merger form on most of the former Chicago & North Western lines, with the exception of the Chicago–Omaha main line. In fact, as of the year 2003, this Overland Route trackage sees more train traffic than ever.

Add in commuter rail services, and the former C&NW line outside of Chicago sees well over 100 trains per day. Although not the subject of this book, the Union Pacific operates the Chicago's former C&NW commuter rail system for Metra, the Windy City's commuter rail system.

As we have seen, intermodal trains and coal train traffic from the West are significant factors on the Overland Route. Both types of traffic have been expanding and growing for the past three decades, and continue to do so under Union Pacific. Train operations are just as exciting as ever, if not more so.

The photos in this chapter illustrate aspects of freight train operations on the former C&NW as they exist following the UP merger. Sadly, as mentioned previously, the C&NW trackage is gone from northern Wisconsin. The Union Pacific operates over the Wisconsin Central (now part of the Canadian National Railway System) and the Burlington Northern Santa Fe (BNSF) to and from Duluth-Superior. Regular freight trains, coal trains, and all-rail ore are the predominant traffic to and from the "North Country."

Finally, it is interesting to note that the Union Pacific is the only "vintage" railroad name remaining after the megamergers of the past few years. In a sense, the Union Pacific has maintained a special tradition dating back to the day of the completion of the first transcontinenal railroad and the Golden Spike celebration of May 1869.

Since the C&NW has played a major role with and for Union Pacific freight and passenger services for many decades, it seems—in a way—only natural for the C&NW to be part of the expanding Union Pacific System.

The C&NW, however, lives on in the hearts of many people with many fond memories. Furthermore, C&NW freight equipment still carries the "CNW" reporting marks along with the Union Pacific shield. With the many different innovations for building freight traffic that were developed by the C&NW, we still have much to learn from that railroad for addressing the future transportation needs of shippers and passengers.

By the time of this 1999 view, four years had passed since the UP-C&NW merger. A westbound time freight rolls through Sauntry (southeast of Superior) on Wisconsin Central trackage (ex-C&NW) en route to Itasca Yard. An SD40-2 still in C&NW paint is leading a UP unit as the train rolls by the pulpwood loading terminal at Sauntry in CTC territory. (Author)

Former C&NW Dash 9-44CW No. 8672 leads an eastbound double-stack train at Mt. Vernon, Iowa, in October 1998. UP retained the C&NW's left-hand running.

UP 9722 meets UP 6346 at Kennard, Nebraska, on Sept. 17, 1995. This is half of a four-train meet at one siding, during UP's period of post-merger congestion.

Former C&NW Dash 8-40C No. 8524 leads a westbound intermodal train near Bertram, Iowa, on the Overland Route in June 1998. (All, William S. Kuba)

left: Another interesting combination on the Overland Route after the merger was the mixture of C&NW and Southern Pacific or Cotton Belt power (both had previously been merged into UP). C&NW SD40-2 No. 6887 leads Cotton Belt GP40-2 No. 7640 on a westbound intermodal train crossing the Mississippi River at Clinton, Iowa, in October 1997.

middle: UP 9722, a GE Dash 9-44CW, leads C&NW power on an eastbound double-stack train crossing the Missouri River Bridge on the Iowa side, shortly after the merger in 1995. (Both, William S. Kuba)

below: All-rail iron ore movements continue to play an important role to and from the "North Country." A UP GE AC4400CW leads an all-rail empty ore train into Itasca Yard in late 2001. The train will be interchanged with the Duluth, Missabe & Iron Range for movement to the Mesabi Range for loading. (Author)

facing page, top: As C&NW rolling stock was repainted after the 1995 merger, the cars retained their CNW reporting marks with a Union Pacific shield, as on covered hopper 96620 in Sept. 2001.

facing page, middle: Another example of this post-merger lettering arrangement is "CenterFlo" covered hopper 175156.

facing page, bottom: Former C&NW covered hopper 438097 was photographed in September 2001.

left: The UP employs a variety of power for switching, including combinations of GP38-2s, GP60s, and so on. GP60 No. 1978 was switching at Superior in late 2000.

bottom: C&NW coal trains operated in and out of Superior, Wis., either on their own line through the eastern part of the city (and then over the DM&IR to the Burlington Northern connection at Saunders), or directly in or out via the BN's ex-Northern Pacific line to and from the coal terminal. This operation continued with Union Pacific. SD90/43MAC No. 8069 leads an empty coal train south on BNSF tracks through Superior's south end, heading for the main line at Central Avenue. The train will then run over the ex-Great Northern line to the Twin Cities. (All, Author)

10
Colorful C&NW

The C&NW's color scheme of yellow and green persisted from its earliest applications to passenger equipment in the 1920s through to the Union Pacific merger in 1995. Although there have been a number of modifications and simplifications over the decades, such as the loss of slogans ("Route of the *400* Streamliners," etc.), and different safety striping applications, the yellow and green remained along with the C&NW insignia.

Many railroads simplified or completely dropped their historical and traditional colors, which in part caused a loss of identity, but this did not happen on the C&NW.

This chapter looks at the C&NW's freight services in color. Even after the Union Pacific merger, yellow remained the dominant color on the former Chicago & North Western lines throughout the Midwest!

above: Two GP50s roll an eastbound inter-modal train through California Junction, Iowa, on July 5, 1980, with top-priority freight for Chicago and eastern destinations. (Lou Schmitz)

left: A GP15-1 and a first-generation roster mate switch at Superior, Wisconsin, on old OmahaRoad trackage at the far eastern end of the Itasca Yard. The photo was taken from the last car of a steam excursion operating between Duluth and South Itasca in September 1984. (Thomas A. Dorin)

above: Four Alco Century units, with No. 4257 in the lead, are laying over at the Ishpeming, Michigan, yard between ore runs in August 1984.

right: As part of a steam excursion and other railroad activities in September 1983, the C&NW lined up a series of freshly painted GP units for display near the Duluth depot.

bottom: Close-up view of GP40 No. 5533 during the September, 1983 display. (All, Thomas A. Dorin)

above: It is May 2, 1985, and an all-rail ore train is heading for Provo, Utah, over the Burlington Northern tracks south of Saunders.

left: Three C&NW units are handling this train with the usual mixture of C&NW, UP, and MoPac cars.

bottom: One of the things that made the all-rail ore trains bound for Utah very interesting was the wide diversity in consists. This train on May 2, 1985, had a UP CA-11 caboose on the rear end. (All, Thomas A. Dorin)

above: During the late 1980s and even into 1990, some of the C&NW all-rail ore trains were powered by vintage EMD GP7s. (Thomas A. Dorin)

right: This 1990 photo shows an empty Minorca pellet train (with C&NW ore cars) arriving at South Itasca, where the train will be interchanged with the DM&IR for movement to Virginia, Minnesota, for loading. (Thomas A. Dorin)

above: This C&NW eastbound loaded coal train consists of Burlington Northern equipment. Led by C&NW No. 5536, the train is rolling east of Meadow Grove, Nebraska, on June 16, 1984. (Lou Schmitz)

left: A loaded ore train heads east over the Partridge Subdivision of what was once known as the Ore Division. The train is en route from the mining area near Eagle Mills to the ore terminal at Escanaba, Mich. (Author)

right: Two trains wait to depart Itasca Yard in January 1986. (Thomas A. Dorin)

below: An empty coal train is headed west at South Morrill, Neb., on September 14, 1991. (Lou Schmitz)

facing page, top: CNWZ Falcon Service trailer 208144, August 15, 1979. (Lou Schmitz)

facing page, middle: CNWZ 202267, August 15, 1979. (Lou Schmitz)

facing page, bottom: C&NW rebuilt a number of ore cars during 1985. (Joe Piersen)

above: The C&NW added extensions to all of its 70-ton ore cars, such as 118867 and the 118635 shown here. The odd thing about the 118867 is the placement of the reporting marks on the extension. The common method was on the car as shown on the 118635. (Author)

right: Former Chicago Great Western work box car X4093 carries CGW reporting marks with the "Employee Owned" slogan. (Thomas A. Dorin)

bottom: C&NW CenterFlo covered hopper 175267 is painted in the gray scheme, while similar cars coupled to it wear the green scheme. (Thomas A. Dorin)

top: CNW hopper car 135799 in a special bicentennial paint scheme, July 3, 1977.

middle: Car 136188 (135800-136299, odd and even numbers) was equipped for rotary dumping. The 53-foot car was at Council Bluffs in 1989.

bottom: Among the last equipment purchased by C&NW prior to the merger were aluminum coal cars like 880063, at Council Bluffs in 1994.

overleaf: Who would have thought that the C&NW would eventually become a major coal hauler—and a coal hauler over long distances? A loaded coal train with GE No. 8647 leading rolls through Dunlap, Iowa, on May 20, 1994. (All, Lou Schmitz)

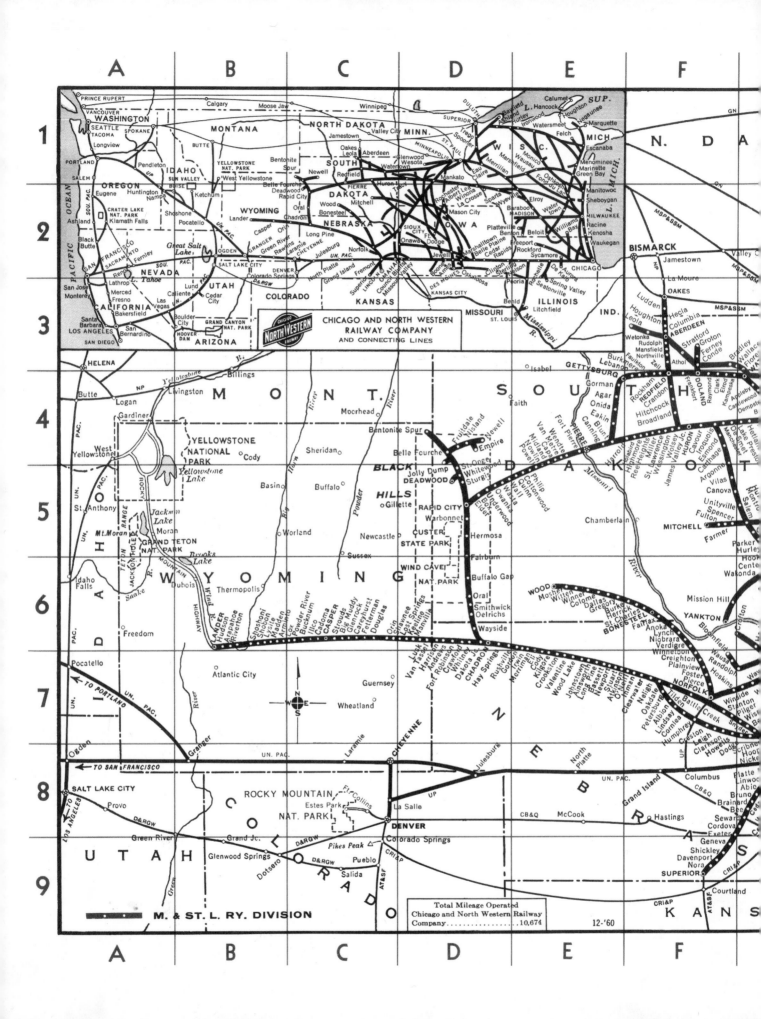